The Dance is an
Animate Composition
in Space. Dancing
is Movement made
Significant; Technique
used to express
Spiritual Content
in Intelligible Form

MARTHA
GRAHAM

MARTHA GRAHAM

THE EARLY YEARS

Edited and with a Foreword by
MERLE ARMITAGE

Illustrated with photographs and
with Carlos Dyer's ink drawings

A DA CAPO PAPERBACK

Library of Congress Cataloging in Publication Data

Armitage, Merle, 1893-1975, ed.
  Martha Graham: the early years.

  (A Da Capo paperback)
  Reprint of the ed. published by M. Armitage,
  Los Angeles.
  1. Graham, Martha — Addresses, essays, lectures.
  [GV1785.G7A7 1978] 793.3'092'4   78-17608
  ISBN 0-306-80084-5 pbk.

ISBN: 0-306-80084-5

First Paperback Edition 1978

This Da Capo Press paperback edition of *Martha Graham:
The Early Years* is an unabridged republication of *Martha Graham*
published in Los Angeles in 1937.

Published by Da Capo Press, Inc.
A Subsidiary of Plenum Publishing Corporation
227 West 17th Street
New York, New York 10011

Martha Graham is unique in her expression
of the fundamentals of life through Dance.
She is one of the world's great artists.

CONTENTS

	Page
Merle Armitage	1
John Martin	7
Lincoln Kirstein	23
Evangeline Stokowski	34
Wallingford Riegger	36
Edith J. R. Isaacs	40
Stark Young	49
Roy Hargrave	54
James Johnson Sweeney	63
George Antheil	71
Louis Danz	78
Martha Graham	83
Margaret Lloyd	89
Affirmations	96
Winthrop Sargeant	111
New York Concerts and Repertoire	118
Concert Tours	124
Special Events	128
Acknowledgements	130

THE PHOTOGRAPHS

Between pages 88 and 89

Ekstasis

Spectre 1914, from "Chronicle"

Portrait With Dyer "Frontier" (by Barbara Morgan)

Prelude to "Transitions"

Spectre 1914

Praeludium II

Frontier

Frontier, Action Photograph

Lamentation, Action Photograph

Sarabande, Action Photograph

Frenetic Rhythm III, Action Photograph

Praeludium I

War, from Suite "Transitions"

Hymn to the Virgin, from "Primitive Mysteries"

"Celebration," Group Dance

Hill Song, from "Horizons"

Act of Judgement, from "American Provincials"

Rehearsal in Studio

Sarabande

Primitive Canticles

Tragic Holiday, from "Chronicle"

Portrait by Edward Biberman

Carlos Dyer "Lamentation"

Louis Horst by Soichi Sunami

● THIS BOOK IS DEDICATED TO LOUIS HORST

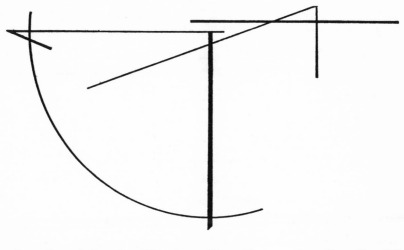

ARMITAGE 1937

No artist fares worse, in the matter of a record of his intentions, than a dancer. The composer has his scores; while the writer, the sculptor, painter and lithographer each work in mediums which are comparatively permanent records of their aesthetic statements and intentions. The one medium which could preserve something of the dancer's art, the cinema, is indifferent.

Although nothing of the evanescent substance of Martha Graham can be captured in a book, something of her meaning can be more or less successfully crystallized in print---the contributors to this volume have accepted this limitation.

At periodic intervals during America's aesthetic adolescence someone was momentarily expected to write the "great American

1

novel." The great American artist was presumed to be a writer or a painter, a third choice being a sculptor. Even as broad an intimation as Isadora Duncan did not prepare us for the appearance of a powerful and authentic American manifestation in the shape of the art of Martha Graham, dancer.

✦ ✦ ✦

Many observers, even those possessing an uncommon knowledge of "the dance" find in Martha Graham much that is strange to them---a world to which they have no key. This is the natural result of what we have seen and experienced, for the dance known in America is exotic. It is Spanish, or it is Russian, or it is pseudo-Oriental, or it is synthetic European folk dance. We have never experienced American dancing, (excluding, of course, the Indian and Negro) and it is incomprehensible to us because we have accepted other civilization's contribution as *the* dance.

Furthermore, the dance of Martha Graham is neither literary (story telling in the allegorical sense) nor is it symbolic. It is a pure art of the dance---a play of form which in itself is significant and provocative---a language of its own, not a handmaiden of another art form. Perhaps it is the first uninfluenced American dance expression, wholly disarming in its simplicity but curiously profound in its complexity.

If certain aspects of her work on first consideration are obscure it may be because she expresses her most profound feeling in a language of her own. More than any other dancer,

2

she makes a real demand upon her audience but no dancer more generously rewards that effort. It seems safe to assume that her fundamental aim is to allow the power and energy of the living world to filter through and animate her work. Her sense of rhythm is the result of this. The word "rhythm" is sometimes used as a substitute for "repetition". But in reality rhythm has little to do with symmetry or balance. Its primary reference is to related movements, the significant movements of life.

In certain of these figures and movements Graham seems to uncover stratas of memory, floating just below consciousness. This is exasperating to a degree because of the beholders' inability to completely recall, or to fully identify, the fragments.

Her imagination frequently conjures forms which seem utterly impossible of plastic realization. Yet by force of conviction and an amazing technique they become highly communicable. She has a singular mastery over life---an almost mesmeric power, and a nobility which demands respect, even if understanding on the part of her auditors is wanting. Everything she does falls under the scrutiny of her own devastating self-criticism ---the severity of which has undoubtedly brought her hours of doubt, discouragement and inner torment.

There are endless theories about the dance, its origins, its early purposes, and its tendencies.

If it is true that the first fear of an infant is that of falling, this sensation must inevitably be bound up with later emotional

3

experiences and can in certain individuals extend into the realm of aesthetics. In analyzing our delight in the quick flight of birds we discovery that it is the "recovery" of the headlong dash which produces in us a sense of exhilaration. Leo Stein believes this "recovery" must be inherent in every medium of expression and has subjected many paintings and other works of art of all periods to this test. Obviously it is potent in the art of the dance and nowhere is it a more natural manifestation than in the performances of Martha Graham. Whether or not this is a conscious thing with her I can not say, nor is it important to know, but the law is there and a confirmation of it.

Both as dancer and choreographer, Martha Graham has an instinctive sense of spacing. She understands the power of understatement, the lift to the imagination in those things not manifest. In her formal designs the *undanced* portions of her choreography are not emptiness---but considered elements of its construction: controlled prolongations.

A growing public has made the discovery that a Martha Graham performance provides almost the best opportunity to see the *contemporary aesthetic* in action. It finds itself traveling over familiar country at an intoxicating speed, usually to mount in the end to new experiences.

Although the motivation of this book is to interpret Martha Graham's relation to the aesthetic of our time in America, and not to deify a person, nevertheless both person, attitude and character must be considered.

One of the first things felt or sensed is her finely organized and disciplined nature. There is in Martha Graham a craving for the perfect synthesis of thought and action---an approach to an ultimate realization, austere and remote. To attend her rehearsals is to realize how agonizingly unattainable is perfection, but she makes no attempt at things beyond her own possibilities. Her sense of proportion is her best counsel. She knows that the more altitude the mind achieves, the greater the pressure on the lines of communication. There is a surprising freedom from the clichés of the dance. Sometimes her meaning in action has the projection of a pitched ball; again she is introspectively powerful, reflecting back only what her audiences can contribute.

Seeing her is to realize the difference between talent and the high order of *her* achievement. Talent is a misused word. It has always seemed to possess dual qualities, the first of which is a natural facility for creation, and the second an attitude which is both individual and particular. Martha Graham adds a further development, a universality and an inner intensity always present in the highest type of creative artist.

Martha Graham has elected her own direction. There is something in her of the crusader and something of the saint. She has a singleness of purpose and a devotion which are the result of fanatical integrity. Privations, ridicule and physical exhaustion have been only incidents in the attainment of definite aims, but she has crystallized something in her dance which could

5

only have happened in this country and which did not mature until now.

What will be the next step in the development of Martha Graham is open to conjecture. The various phases of revolt which have been so fruitful, could lead to a not illogical, even if unsuspected, evolution. A neo-classic period could be of the utmost importance in focusing the dance of tomorrow. Martha Graham's neo-classicism would in a sense be a magnificent development as her next manifestation; a crystallization, a concentration of forces, a point of departure for the inevitable succeeding progression.

MARTIN   1 9 3 7

The following dated extracts from John Martin's Reviews (see acknowledgments) are reprinted by permission of John Martin and the New York Times.

Each successive appearance of Martha Graham makes more emphatic the conclusion that she is a unique figure in the American dance. It is easy to understand how one might dislike her work intensely; it is considerably easier to understand how

7

one might like it with equal intensity and be stimulated and disturbed by it. The only unimaginable reaction would be indifference.

Those who stay away from her concerts offer certain valid reasons for so doing, and some who go because they are interested in spite of themselves share the view. It is held against her, for example, that she is "arty" and precious and solemn; that she belongs to what one of her colleagues delights to call "the morbid moderns"; that she has turned her back on the dance and her face toward the theatre; that her compositions are all in one key and her programs monotonous. To which accusations there is no reply except, "What of it?"

It would be a hopeless task to undertake the refutation of such criticisms, for they are too largely true to admit of being argued out of the way. But such a merely partial catalogue tells only a small fraction of the tale. Through the haze of these items of debit glows the light of one of the few extraordinary talents of the day; and sometimes the very haze itself provides points of shadow that serve to heighten the design.

Audiences who come to be amused and entertained will go away disappointed, for Miss Graham's programs are alive with passion and protest, and are couched in a vein to freighten away somnolescence. If the passion of her dances is not of the turbulent and unbridled order, it nevertheless burns with the slow and deadly fire of the intellect. She does the unforgivable thing for a dancer to do---she makes you think; yet it is thinking of a peculiar character, for it is less of the brain than of some organ absent from anatomical charts, that reacts to aesthetic stimuli. She leaves you upheaved and disquieted and furnishes afterthoughts not calculated to soothe such a condition.

Frequently the vividness and intensity of her purpose are so potent that on the rise of the curtain they strike like a blow, and in that moment one must decide whether he is for or against her. He either recoils and steels himself against further attacks or accepts her challenge and prepares to indulge in a friendly sparring match. If one tries to sit limp and inactive, the consequences are obvious.

Miss Graham deals more and more in essences. She boils down her moods and movements until they are devoid of all extraneous substances and are concentrated to the highest degree. She gives less and less of the full dimensions of her meanings; she indicates, she suggests, she leads you on with her. And because she is so sparing it is not difficult to follow along; there are no sidetracks and byways.

Unlike her own dance compositions, she does not develop in a direct line. She is a constant surprise. Even when she repeats her dances on consecutive programs they are filled with new colors, and sometimes with new designs; they have been pruned and trimmed and even reoriented. One of her strongest attributes is her capacity for self-criticism and her willingness to revise and discard. This makes for confusion when one attempts to prognosticate.

9

And she is not one to shrink from adventure. It is rarely that audiences are given the opportunity to watch such vigorous experimentation as she provides, backed by a technical proficiency and an artistic equipment which gives her the right to try out new ideas. The interesting question which arises out of this constant variation in style and content is whether she is passing through a period of unsettlement and will eventually find the ground upon which she wishes to stand or whether she has already found herself and that self is one which must be incessantly in a state of change in order to create with vitality.

1929

◆　◆　◆

Miss Graham is an individualist to the last degree in her artistic convictions, and one who finds compromise the most difficult thing to approach when the principles for which she stands are involved. As is apparently inevitable in such a case, she has incurred enmities as well as evoked adulation; that she has been able to keep her head between the two augurs well for the future.

It is no longer possible, however, to place Miss Graham's achievement entirely in the future; she has already touched the borderland of that mystic territory where greatness dwells. That she has not yet received the accolade from the general public cannot be explained altogether by the fact that she has sometimes missed the ultimate perfection in her art. Personally, she is at the furthest point from flambuoyance, and seems to give no attention to the business of self-exploitation. Perhaps she feels that her ardent disciples err too seriously in that direction already. The fact of being a prophet in her own country also has undoubtedly affected the popular verdict; it is like having a genius in the family to form part of the audience which watches an artist grow up. There is every reason to believe that a fuller recognition of her unique powers would be granted by a strange public---in Germany, for example, where such things are of deeper interest than they have yet become in America.

Miss Graham has rarely failed to produce an effect, but it has not been one of warmth and elevation, but rather of tension and disturbed thinking. The reason for this is readily apparent in retrospect. With a basic theory of dancing that was the reverse of public conviction, her position was one which offered only two modes of conduct: either she must back gracefully out of the road she had put her foot to or she must stiffen her lip and march aggressively forward. When, after several years of hard fighting she had made a sufficient number of converts, there began to be noticeable a change of attitude in her own work as well as in the response of her audience. She had found something she could lean upon.

The first note of gentleness and wistfulness was sounded in her dance called "Adolescence". Now in the "Primitive Mysteries" it has reached its highest point thus far. Here is a composition which must be ranked among the choreographic masterpieces of the modern dance movement. Its simplicity of form and its evocation of the childlike religious elevation of a primitive people never falter for a moment . . . Miss Graham's performance, considered apart from the excellencies of her composition, is one of warmth and graciousness, and in this she is seconded on every side by her group.

In this emotional blossoming Miss Graham's technique likewise bears the mark of change. She has built her physical system upon the basis of percussive movement---a stroke of muscular effort and its consequent vibrations of recovery. In her earlier and more defensive compositions it was a stroke that assumed the chief importance, while the aftertones were allowed to take care of themselves. Now, without having violated in the least the canons of the method, she has found the secret of striking without clangor, like the stroke of those mellow gongs of the Orient which begin their vibrations as if without an initial percussion.

Certain particular units find themselves repeated frequently in various compositions, but they are continually supplemented by other units which appear to have arisen for the first time in the dancer's experience. To say that they are invented gives the impression of ingenuity, which is far from the case; to say that they are created also implies the making of something out of nothing, which is equally untrue. They are perhaps more nearly discovered, as the result of emotional experiences which evolve their own expression through the channels of a responsive body.

In arranging these movements into form, Miss Graham has developed a style that has much in common with modern painting and sculpture. It is economical of means, though no longer scanty, and eliminates all but the very essentials. It is strong of accent, and consequently distorted. It credits its audience with the ability to respond to esthetic impulses and never stoops to platitude or explanation. When it has furnished the suggestion, the onlooker is counted upon to supply the completion of the experience in his own receptiveness.

For the same reasons, therefore, that modern music and modern painting have had such an uphill road to travel in the winning of public sympathy, Miss Graham's dancing seems obscure and ludicrous to those who use dance recitals as a substitute for bridge parties and backgammon. Certainly when the time arrives in which dancing is clearly seen to be no more a phase of "show business" than symphonic music is, a large portion of the credit will fall to the share of this unswerving modernist who is at last beginning to come into her own.

1931

✦　✦　✦

To evaluate Miss Graham's contribution to the arts, or even to participate in the experience of her highly individual estheticism, it is necessary to follow her with the deepest attention in everything she does. To miss a single performance is to risk the omission of an essential link between those changes of style and approach which follow one another in rapid succession.

It is unfortunate that this should be so; it would be eminently desirable if Miss Graham could hitch her Pegasus on each peak and dismount long enough for the rest of us to accomplish the climb and get our breath. Such a course, however, is apparently impossible, not because of deliberate perversity, which is sometimes held to characterize her creative conduct, but because of the degree of sensitivity which belongs to her mind and the rapidity with which it absorbs and digests the influence of new experiences.

When the now famous "Dithyrambic" had its first performance in December, 1931, it was the expressed hope of this writer that in spite of the magnitude of the composition it would not be repeated too often or followed by too many others of its kind. Miss Graham, herself, after this first performance, was doubtful that she would ever dance it again. But this proved to be a matter not of choice but of necessity. Whatever had given rise to the composition of "Dithyrambic" had so taken hold of the composer she could not shake it off at will. It made itself felt in everything that followed . . . this influence had completely captured the ground and another new Martha Graham was revealed to replace all the other new Martha Grahams of the past.

It is perhaps a little unfair to treat Miss Graham's admirable plasticity of mind thus as a sort of lifelong proteanism; for just as surely as she will continue to alter and shift her course, just so surely will she continue to reveal that nucleus of her art which is essentially constant. This central core becomes sounder and solider with each advancing phase, throwing off what is by nature transient and retaining what is vital and fundamental.

Like the dance of the American Indian by which she has been deeply inspired, Miss Graham's dance is one toward integration. She has turned her back equally on the impertinences of "self-expression" and on the indulgences of that theory which seeks in the dance a release from reality. There is evident in her progressions thus far a purpose to identify herself with reality, to pierce through all the strata of the trivial to the roots of human experience.

The change, therefore, from the strong primitive influences of the Indian period which preceded "Dithyrambic" and the present period which is suggestive of pre-Aeschylean Greek is not as great a one as it might appear. The link between the two periods is perhaps to be found in the group of four "Dance Songs". This is in effect a restatement of the materials of the longer and earlier "Ceremonials"; its background is unmistakably Indian, but its treatment departs completely from the comparative elaborations of the compositions of the Indian period and takes on the extreme simplification which characterizes such newer compositions as "Tragic Patterns", and more especially the exquisite "Ekstasis."

Simplification can scarcely be called a new development for Miss Graham, yet there is something decidedly new about her present use of it. In the earlier phase of her work she was

15

frequently and justly taken to task for her sparseness; now such a criticism is quite unfounded. Though she draws with an even finer line, she can no longer be accused of understatement. Her fineness is a result not of penuriousness but of concentration.

1933

✦   ✦   ✦

In the new cycle "Dances of Possession" it is no longer possible to doubt that the dancer has entered upon a new phase of her art. This has long ago ceased to be a surprise to those who have followed Miss Graham's work with the attention it rightly demands, for, like every living organism, her dancing is ever in the process of change and development. As one of her colleagues once remarked of a new program, "Whenever she changes she proves herself right." . . . Miss Graham, for all her incessant and almost restless variation of manner and method, does not change casually or easily. She refuses, indeed, to do anything that does not completely convince her of its necessity. For example, on several occasions during the past few seasons she has stated in public lectures her reasons for the sparing use of the hands which has been so characteristic of her work. She feels, she has said, that the hands are the last members of the body to be developed, and the comparison of their use in crude and unpolished eras will uphold this theory.

For herself, she could not use her hands arbitrarily just to keep them busy, but must allow their use to grow naturally as the demand for it came from within. Perhaps nothing in a recent

16

performance was more significant than that the hands were beginning to participate in small but indicative measure . . .

Martha Graham's dancing is essentially religious in its character. Not that it deals in symbols of piety or moral preachments, but that it concerns itself with the individual and his contacts with the forces of the universe. In this it restores the dance to the high estate from which it fell when it became merely a pastime for an idle aristocracy.

It is undoubtedly this quality which produces in the spectator such violent reactions, whether of delight or horror. Sometimes, as in the deep loveliness of the second "fragment" of "Ekstasis" or in the orgiastic abandon of "Dithyrambic", Miss Graham is concerned with rituals of worship; at other times she bends her energies to the casting out of devils. The latter is obviously her purpose in the new "Frenetic Rhythms". The grotesque animality of its first dance, the pseudo-Oriental auto-intoxication of the second dance, and the arrant vulgarity of the third dance, all are treated as devils to be exorcised. And if they can stand against such a ritual they are devils of colossal strength!

1933

✦ ✦ ✦

Of the "American Provincials" there is an altogether different account to be rendered. Here is a superb achievement, almost as much of the theatre as of the dance. Its first section, "Act of Piety", captures the essence of the ferocious Puritan tradition as it is rarely captured. It is a subject so often played with that

17

it had become dangerously trite, but here it bursts forth with such new depths and such fresh inspiration that it becomes a truth told as for the first time. Miss Graham never for one instant condescends to her subject. She measures it at its full value. There is no ridicule, no easy taunting at a dead victim. Her Puritan is a worthy enemy, a creature of heroic proportions.

The dance draws a close parallel between this kind of masochistic piety and the orgiastic religious ritual of the savage. It is part sex, part pride, part terror and all frenzy. It is nothing that could be plastered onto the surface of any individual whatever his creed or confession. It has nothing of hypocrisy or superficiality, but is an all too genuine exudation of primitive passion. Though it is in every sense an American study, it is also something larger. It is, indeed, that concept without time or place which the Greeks called Medea. And what a Medea Miss Graham could play if she chose to put her mind to it !

In the second part of the dance, after a tremendous and inevitable exit of the solo figure, the group, which has stood scarcely visible at the sides, becomes the centre of the picture. The movement is entitled, "Act of Judgment", and is as cruel and pitiless a composition as such a title would naturally connote in such a dance. With a sort of poetic compensation the crowd now has its day. It deals its malign justice upon its victim, but she, like some regal New England Gorgon, stands at the end defiant and essentially unconquered. There is apparently no resolution to such a conflict. Euripides knew that when he carried off his Medea, both victorious and defeated, in a dragon chariot.

In an earlier work, the beautiful "Heretic", Miss Graham has dealt with something of the same matter, but in an entirely different way. There with stark impersonality she pictured the persecution of an obviously superior individual by a vindictive and stupid mob. Though it also leans in the direction of the theatre, it is far more pure dance in its economy and its greater abstraction. At first sight the two dances are closely related, but there is a world of difference in their treatment and in their ultimate effect.

In "American Provincials" one can scarcely fail to see an addition to that list of dances in Miss Graham's repertoire which have about them the air of permanence. "Heretic" was perhaps the first of the number, though at least one observer still clings to memories of the lovely "Adolescence" as a possible predecessor. The "Primitive Mysteries" is certainly another item in the list. It is possible to choose several others, such as "Lamentation" and "Celebration" and the "Sarabande" and perhaps "Frenetic Rhythms", but about these there is possible a difference of opinion. There seems less chance for disagreement about "American Provincials" or at least the "Act of Piety", among any who accept Miss Graham's art at all. For those who quite honestly find themselves unable to do so, one cannot resist a heartfelt regret, as each admirable composition is added to her repertoire.   1934

✦   ✦   ✦

19

Martha Graham continues to be the outstanding paradox in the dance world. This proves, if it proves anything at all, how an artist who is original and creative (to use the much abused words in their strictest sense) reduces the smug formulas of the aesthetes to so many incoherent absurdities. Such a conclusion, to be sure, is nothing more than a platitude for practically every great artist, in whatever line, has produced the same confusion among the orthodox.

When it happens, however, in the biographies of the acknowledged masters, it is far easier to recognize for what it is than when it is seen taking place under one's very eyes in the experience of a contemporary artist, whose personal attributes have not yet been transfigured by the effulgence of academic acceptance.

1934

✦ ✦ ✦

. . . A choreographic setting of Edgar Varese' "Integrales", sub-titled "Shapes of Ancestral Wonder" . . . was another triumph. . . . It is quite literally an astounding piece of work. Built in huge architectural terms, it is essentially dealing in abstractions, yet they are somehow so terrifically energized that the effect is one of sweeping emotion. 1934

✦ ✦ ✦

Entirely without affectation or striving "Frontier" is deeply felt and simply projected. In addition it is blessed with a full and beautiful musical setting by Louis Horst and an extremely effective bit of decor by Isamu Noguchi. Here, one believes, Miss

20

Graham has touched the finest point of her career, and only an audience of wooden Indians could fail to be moved by it.   1935

♦   ♦   ♦

When the definitive history of the dance comes to be written it will become evident that no other dancer has yet touched the borders to which she has extended the compass of movement. Not only in a technical sense, though here too she has proved the body capable of a phenomenal range, but especially in the field of creative expressional movement has she made an incomparable contribution.   1936

♦   ♦   ♦

Not since the eloquent and beautiful "Frontier" first presented three seasons ago, has Miss Graham given us anything half so fine as "Immediate Tragedy". Though its subject matter, dealing as it does with contemporary Spain, is removed half-way around the world from the early American milieu of "Frontier", there is something that the two dances possess in common. Perhaps it is their spirit of dedication; perhaps it concerns also their simplicity of form and the transparent elements of which they are built.

Lest there may be something of the suggestion of "propaganda" or of mere timeliness about a theme deriving from the Spanish War, let it be said at once that this will be a moving dance long after the tragic situation in Spain has been brought to a conclusion, for it has completely universalized its materials. Indeed, neither its title nor its subtitle, "Dance of Dedication",

21

has a word to say about any specific happening or locale. It is a picture of fortitude, especially of woman's fortitude; of the acceptance of a challenge with a kind of passionate self-containment. From its emotional quality one recognizes its source rather than through any external means.

To be sure, there is a touch of Spain in the costume, if only the merest hint; there is also an occasional bit of movement which presents the magnificent dignity of the Spanish woman as we know her through her dance. Again, Henry Cowell's deeply poignant music with its persistent phrase is couched in the measure of the sarabande. But the work communicates its meaning far less by any of these surface aids than by the innate power of evocation which belongs to Martha Graham. In this great gift she is surpassed by no other artist of our time, and "Immediate Tragedy" finds her at her best.   1937

K I R S T E I N   1 9 3 7

Perhaps a skillful draughtsman could do it, or a painter. Someone with an evocative connection between their memory, their present eye, and a sharp hand that could put it down for someone else to see. Otherwise it is impossible to give another person any idea of the difference between what Martha Graham looked like to me when I first began to see her and what she seems to me now. I cannot assume that the change is entirely

23

with me or entirely with her. But there is a very great change and I submit my analysis of it because I think it is not an uncommon experience for some of the people who have watched her for the last seven years.

Even then she seemed strong, so strong in fact that I could only with the greatest difficulty look at her at all. I saw her as a sort of rigid embodiment of a principle I did not wish to understand. I felt her as an arrogant and blind assertion of gesture and movement which were both repellent in themselves, and based on some substructure as capricious as it was sterile. What I considered to be her brand of stark hysteria antagonized my sympathy, and her exhaustingly arbitrary invention angered my eyes. I left her concerts, to which I could not but continue to go, irritated to the point of exasperation and physically worn out. I told this to one of her earliest and most powerful admirers. He nodded his head like a diagnostician, and said 'Exactly', as if it was sure proof of some toxin working. I was suspicious of it just as I would be suspicious of some active and inexplicable energy which was not an immediate personal threat but which might be the demonstration of some power I had best beware of since I could not be sure how it would next affect me. It worried me like a headache. Her wiry concentration, her awkward, jarring idiosyncrasies and stammering activity repelled me so strongly that I was continually drawn back to see her almost to exorcise myself of curiosity, or to lay the ghost of all the irritating questions which raised themselves when I watched her.

24

Why was all this so violent? I was very accustomed to dancing, and it had long been my first interest. Perhaps that was just the reason. I was brought up on the Russian Ballet, and I had an exclusive and obsessive passion for it. I had not seen enough dancing to know that not only were there other kinds of dancing, but that the Russian Ballet at that time was a dilute replica of an original intention, and that its later developments were decorative survivals depending on shocks from many extraneous sources other than dancing, to keep it alive. I had not seen the original Russian Ballet of 1909 to 1919. My first experience of it was the post-war period of 1923 when the School of Paris had displaced the original Russian collaborators, and when Diaghilev was in the full throes of the cubist revolution. It was all extremely theatrical, physically stimulating and violently opposed to the accepted exotic complacencies of 'Scheherezade', 'Cleopatre', or 'Prince Igor'. It made no difference that the dancing was only a little less important than the music, and that the painters' portion---the dresses and the decor, were the real excuse for the whole show, which was, in essence, anti-theatrical and anti-choreographic.

So, when I first saw Graham, I mistook her attitude, confused her approach, and decided it was all very old-fashioned, provincial, unresourceful and ultimately uninteresting in comparison to the urbane sights and sounds, the perverse, acid disharmonies and nervous excitement then active in the disintegration of the classic tradition of the ballet. I went to Graham expecting to be shocked further than by the collaborations of Picasso, Cocteau and Massine. I was unequipped for her simplicity and self-blinded to her genuinely primitive expression. For me the primitive was the primitivistic, the Stravinsky of *Sacre* and *Noces,* with all their attendant resources of complex colour, historic reference and elaborate orchestration. The archaic was the archaistic of the 'Afternoon of a Faun'; the contemporary was the chic of *'Parade'* or *'Les Biches'.* This solitary dancer, not even a girl, with her Spartan band of girls seeming to me to press themselves into replicas of the steel woman she was, appeared either naive or pretentious, which, I could never fully decide. But the force of the personality of the woman magnetized me continually.

It is the theatrical aspect of dancing that attracts me most, and it was her specifically conceived work for the theatre that first overcame my blanket resistance to her. After seeing the dances in Katherine Cornell's 'Romeo and Juliet', and after watching rehearsals for the living choral frieze in John Houseman's production of MacLeish's 'Panic', I felt I had a nucleus of comprehension, or at least satisfaction in her work which might, in time, absolve me from further hate. By that time my long love affair with the Russian Ballet had resolved itself in something less than an affectionate friendship, and my dissatisfaction with the heirs of Diaghilev opened my mind, of necessity, to other possibilities for dancing. Seeing Wigman as a soloist, and later as a composer, however, further momentarily confused me.

Somehow I expected a corroboration of my original opinion of Graham in watching Wigman. What I actually felt was her enormous difference from the American, and chiefly that assertion of blind, vague, quasi-mystical self-expressionism which is the unfortunate universal heritage of the descent from Wagner. Yet my own acumen was insufficiently skilled to reconcile the difference between Graham and Wigman. Certain superficial similarities, such as the use of percussion, furthered a confusion already aggravated by an instinctive concept of their genuine opposition.

The rest of the history of my larger comprehension of Graham is too subjective to be of much interest and would involve autobiographical rationalization, half-truth and accident which is interesting only to the writer. To admit the element of a gradual revelation by unfrightened eyes would be nearer the truth and just as logical. Yet I cannot pretend that where once I thought was all blackness has become in a flash, all light. I believe that in Graham's work of five and six years ago there were still elements of her own unachieved revolt, unassimilated and inorganic, which coincided with those insecure and immature philosophies of Spenglerian decay and European snobbery with which I was then equipped and which colored my opinion of her art. The lack of necessity for a continuation of that particular energy imperative in an artist's first personal revolt brings a breadth and freedom impossible and even undesirable in earlier stages. The concentration demanded to cleanse inertia from any tradition or form is seldom attractive and often as repulsive as the dead growth for which it is the specific antidote. But this concentration remains nervous, and after it has won its fight can exert itself into a calmer and more expansive activity.

To write descriptions of dancing is even more aimless than to paint pictures of music. One can at least quote musical phrases or point to a handy phonograph. Most photographs are intrinsically as subjective and unsatisfactory as dance criticism, and the so-called 'candid' camera is the greatest trickster of all. So far the films have given us no hint of the record for which we hope with some confidence. So to write about Martha Graham's dances would be only interesting if the writer was the equivalent of his subject. It is a pity that the public is so prone to take what they are given from the daily unequipped and undigested press, yet one cannot flatly decide there is no valid place for writing about dancing. One is much struck by reading William Butler Yeats' vindication of his drastic editing of Wilde's 'Ballad of Reading Goal': He simply said his own position as a poet permitted it. This proud statement is irrefutable. We are interested in seeing Dunoyer de Segonzac's or even Bourdelle's drawings of Isadora Duncan, but who takes the trouble to read the 'Appreciation' of even such genial critics as Huneker or H. T. Parker. They seem like the quaint testimonials of lovers. Even a great poet's opinion, like Gauthier's rhapsodies to Fanny Ellsler or Taglioni only serve to cause a lifetime's vain work for scholars. What were they *really* like? The most one can do about Graham is to see her. The seeing is at once the supreme satisfaction and the principal praise. The quality so powerful in the visionary realm of space is dilute in speech and faint in print. When Ruth St. Denis or Shan-Kar or Kreutzberg speak of Graham, one can listen with respect. What Isadora would think of her would be fascinating. That Toumanova admires her is interesting, and yet . . .

And yet one must say something, not exactly for the record, not even for one's children who are doomed to the same questions we share about the last generation, but rather as one leaves the theatre saying to people we don't even know---'Wasn't it wonderful'.

The dance and the dramatic stage are pre-eminently the fields of creative art in which women have equalled and can surpass men on their own terms. Three American women have meant more to contemporary dancing than any other three women of any nation, and one can almost say as much as any three other men. Ruth St. Denis showed a new conglomerate nation the dance idioms of all its component peoples in a form which they could credit with intensity and dignity, and she laid the foundation for an interest in the possibility of theatrical dancing on a continent which had suffered from the blasts of puritan hatred for a frank and fluent physicality. Isadora, by the large assertion of her personal vision, gave the idea, if not the form, of dance as an unassailable position for serious endeavor, in terms of an immediate necessity. Martha Graham, in developing a usable technique and a powerful presence, has employed not merely the exotic cultures of the world, nor the vision of a past perfection, but she has, on their foundation, erected a personal classicism and a contemporary expression suitable and equal to her place and time.

Graham's whole achievement is forcefully apparent over the last year. Her technical usages seem as well forged as the group of dancers who have been trained to demonstrate them. The story of her heroic struggle against all sorts of resentments and inertia is very fragmentarily echoed in such opposition as my own. As proof of her arrival, of that arrival free of the necessity to attack further the immediate sources from which she has sprung, and free to create works in the scope of a serene maturity, are two large facts, increasingly obvious. The first is the least important, but it has its interest. Graham is considered almost an academy by certain dancers and dance enthusiasts who, appreciating her present work, have forgotten the fifteen years of varied experiment, rejection and influence which have gone into smelting her ore into its present ingot. They forget the years of theatrical experience, the time with Denishawn, the investigation of Greece, Mexico, and our own South West, the French Gothic, the Far East, and every technical device or innovation available to a dancer. And so when Graham emerges with a new direction or even an accentuation, an extension of an old one, they sometimes accuse her of a change which seems to them a betrayal. They have decided what kind of movement they will expect from her, and if this tendency is not demonstrated as orthodox, she is declared her own first heretic. It was not the most comforting of cynics who said that he loved his friends but he adored his enemies. Every strong artist can resist the head-on attack of their convinced opponents, but the impatient solicitude and insinuating pressure of admirers is even harder to take, particularly when they personally identify one aspect only in the admired artist with the entirety of their admiration.

The other and far more important testimonial of Graham's immediate situation is the work she has presented in the last two years. The pieces for her group are longer, more varied and grow more as dramas danced than as fragmentary dramatic dances. She is the protagonist against a background of her group that is sometimes choral, and sometimes a group that collectively complements her as a balancing soloist. Her use of decor even when it is not completely successful as with the 'Mobiles' of Calder, or Noguchi's forms, shows her intention of presenting a synthesis refusing none of the responsibilities that the theatre offers. The two straight lines that point herself against the segment of the fence-rails in 'Frontier' are at once cleanly suggestive and helpful to her dance, enlarging the perspective and at the same time centering her on the stage which is broad plains and a sector of the globe.

It is distressing and confusing to invoke nationalistic qualities as a preeminent value in an artist's essence today, particu-

31

larly when every praise of nationalism seems an affront and a threat to a wider understanding of the peoples of the earth who are fighting to keep their integrity as human beings against the pressure of Fascism. But Martha Graham has a specifically American quality which cannot be ignored and which must be apparent to everyone. It is not a red, white and blue patriotic exuberance, nor even the naive free-blown boundlessly hopeful openness of the young continent which Europeans always professed to see in Isadora. America has become middle-aged, if not mature in the last twenty years. Graham's connection with our continent is less racial than essential and geographical. She has in 'Frontier' much of the courage of Whitman's unachieved dream, but she has also a more realistic and present spirit. By now she has presupposed the ferocious, bland, hysterical puritanism of 'Act of Piety' and 'Act of Judgment' which Hawthorne would have so completely recognized. She has created a kind of candid, sweeping and wind-worn liberty for her individual expression at once beautiful and useful, like a piece of exquisitely realized Shaker furniture or homespun clothing.

Artists working today are not ignorant of the scope of times through which they live. There have been few occasions in modern history when, due to recent advances in communications and the scientific interpretation of history, artists have been so conscious of their position in relation to the large events smashing around them. But there are very few of these artists, however sincere, who either from lack of skill, talent or concentration, have been equal to the material with which their times provide them. When Martha Graham presented 'Immediate Tragedy' she made a keystone masterpiece of the same powerful wave-length as the concatenation of energies operating throughout the world today. The news from Spain in daily cables alternately frightens and thrills us. The battle of Spain is *the* immediate tragedy of our lives, far more so than the Great War. In her dance we do not think of Graham as an exponent of the 'modern' dance, or even of dancing at all. But only by the dance can such an intense, clear and sweeping vision be inscribed. In it she is an artist who can presuppose not only a technical mastery which is now triumphantly universal as it was once aggressively personal, but she is also a conscious creator who has resolved the atmosphere of Spanish history from the Inquisition to Guernica, the temperature of violence and pride, that staggering human pride in which she has erased the means of her art to give us a positive declaration, a revelation of catastrophe and ultimate control.

33

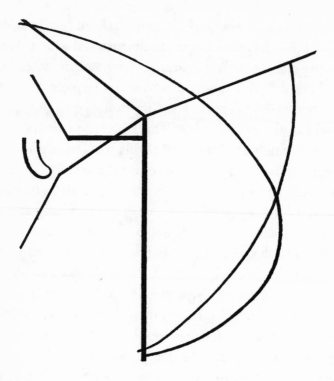

STOKOWSKI 1937

"She is an avatar"---was Uday Shankar's remark when he saw Martha Graham dance. This proof of the universality of Miss Graham's art adds to the conviction that here is a dancer of astonishing force and power whose motivation transcends a local idiom and expresses a planetary idea.

34

In "Frontier" for example Miss Graham steps from the American scene into lucid abstraction where one can feel one's own mind pushing against the horizon of its limitations and expanding in a new and altogether stimulating manner. The frontier she dances becomes any and all frontiers, physical or mental---due to this remarkable power of Miss Graham to portray the universal through the particular. That art is essentially attitudinal in its essence and can make us feel and understand more deeply whatever it portrays---this artist demonstrates by her genius.

One feels that with the phenomenon of Martha Graham the American dance comes of age.

R I E G G E R   1 9 3 7

My first meeting with Martha Graham was after a New York recital of hers in 1928, when, impressed with her art---to me it was like a revelation---I went back-stage to become one of a line waiting to shake her hand.

So far as I know, the first work of mine that Miss Graham heard was the Study in Sonority at a Pro Musica concert in

March, 1930. In the fall of that year she asked me to consult with her about music for a new dance, "Bacchanale". When I arrived at her studio I found to my surprise her dance group assembled and ready to perform for me the already completed dance. Thus I became party to nearly the first attempt at writing music to a dance already composed,---I say nearly for at this time Louis Horst was writing music for Primitive Mysteries.

My next collaboration with Miss Graham was in Frenetic Rhythms the following year. It was not until the fall of 1936 that she was ready to call on me for her first large dance creation based on a social theme, war, and the portrayal of the causes and effects of war in terms of human reaction, with finally the exhortation to the attainment of a world in which war would be forever banished. "Chronicle" is the choreographic embodiment of the most eloquent sermon, the most searching analysis, the most scathing indictment of the great scourge of mankind.

It is hard to evaluate objectively Miss Graham's art. Watching her in rehearsal or at one of her classes, there seems to be no technical phase of dancing in which she is surpassed by her contemporaries. Those dancers who depend on virtuosity seem here outclassed in every respect, and yet with Miss Graham technic is never obtruded, never an end in itself.

Miss Graham's art has been called abstract, yet in every gesture the human equation is present, never in a formalized way, always as an organic element. She is a true apostle of the "modern" in doing away with the fripperies of a bygone age, stripping art down to the essentials. This process had taken place in the other arts; it was Graham's world contribution to accomplish it in the dance.

With Graham the act of creating is a long and painful one. It is hard for one who sees the finished product, so authentic in its final form, to imagine the slow evolution, the merciless self-discipline involved. The same unyielding will to perfection is infused by her into her dance group, who are willing to put forth superhuman effort for one who never spares her own self in the achievement of artistic ends.

The tragedy of Miss Graham's art is that like all dancing it is bound up with time and space, that is, ephemeral unless it can in some way be fixed. And here we find the same indifference to waste that is so common to the American scene. Is her sublime art to go in a few short years the way of Isadora Duncan's and be a mere tradition? Are we to lose forever her present and future repertoire as we have already lost *Dithyrambics, Ceremonials, Integrales* and others of her matchless creations, now definitely abandoned? The composer writes a score which future generations may play. The art of dancers is literally "interred with their bones".

Dance notation, which has recently received such an impetus, is concerned only with the objective elements that go to make up the dance, the analysis and recording of motion, balance, position, design, posture, etc. Assuming for it the highest degree of accuracy, how can one by this method project a great personality? How the surpassing subtlety that is Graham's, her poetry of motion, her physiognomy, extraordinary, haunting, the embodiment of ageless tragedy? Clearly we owe it to ourselves and to all posterity to preserve these priceless things by the best means at our disposal, the sound film. What would we not give today to be able to see Duncan, Pavlova, and now Argentina on the screen!

These things we know yet we do nothing. Last summer witnessed another interment, *Sarabande,* anachronism in name only and pure Graham, now apparently to be given no more.

To permit these art casualties to take place in our midst is an act of passive vandalism which future ages will never forgive. What art superior to Graham's has America given to the world? Where else is to be found such distillation of sheer beauty, such economy yet wealth of means, such mastery of technique, clarity of thinking?

Makers of Hollywood films will not be interested in Graham as a commercial venture. Art speculators did not outbid one another for the paintings of van Gogh and Cézanne. Clearly other ways must be found, and quickly, of salvaging Graham's art. What is to be done?

I S A A C S   1 9 3 7

The pioneer in the arts who sets out to cut a new road for himself and his fellows usually finds a larger task than he expects, however brave and adventurous and far-seeing he may be. A path into new forms of art cannot be surveyed and engineered in advance like a new highway. The artist may know well the direction he desires to take, but he can seldom figure his exact goal in advance, or know how far he must go to reach it. Each new

40

obstacle down, each new levelling of an old prejudice or an out-worn tradition, may open an unexpected vista, not into freedom but into more obstacles. That is why art pioneering is so hazard-ous and so often unhappily unrewarding. The artist who tries it is apt in his enthusiasm to weary himself in the search and to wear himself down to a point where creation is no longer possible for him. Only real genius can withstand the rigors of the life. If this is true of the painter, the poet, the novelist, it is doubly true of the dancer, who must use himself as the material for his own experiments.

It has been a great good fortune that this age of ours, which is the age of dance pioneering in America, has had Martha Graham among its leaders. She is endlessly curious and enquir-ing. She is never satisfied---for long---with anything she does. There seems never, for her, to be an end of any road. Her method of pressing forward is not the passive but the active way; it is always by dancing through a problem first, and thinking through it afterward---the hardest way there is, but the way of the true artist.

For the dancers of all times there have been three funda-mental points of departure: the age in which they live, the space through which they move, the body with which they move. The three are closely interrelated. The age in which a dancer lives dictates to a large extent the material and the use of his dance ---whether it is a religious, theatrical, social or personal expres-sion, or something of each. Through its architecture, it influ-

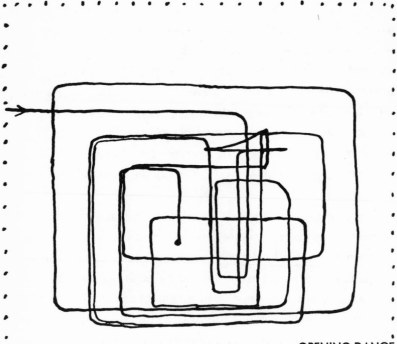

OPENING DANCE

ences the form and scale of the space which a dancer uses for his performance---the arena, the stage, the space before the altar, the village green, the dance hall. And even more by its habits of living and style of dress, it shapes the dancer's body.

When the formalities and graces of life at court were an ideal of beauty and a standard of taste, the lovely formal patterns marked by a dance along a palace floor---the labyrinth and spiral, the rose and double-rose, the vines and flower clusters---

42

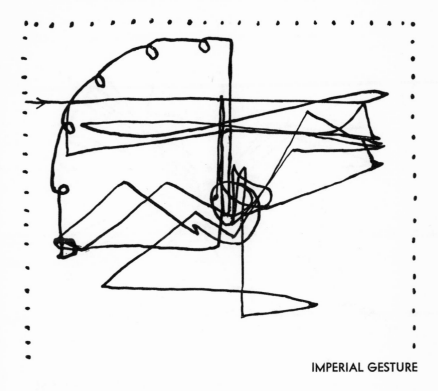

IMPERIAL GESTURE

were a part of the record of the life itself. There was no spiritual elevation in the dances, no effort to free the dancers from the earth on whose smoothed surfaces they walked, only the desire to keep the pattern on the floor clear and dignified and beautiful.

Society has gone a long way from that day to this, and the dance has sometimes foreshadowed social change and sometimes followed in its wake. But there seems to be no such thing as a static period in a dance that is alive in a live world.

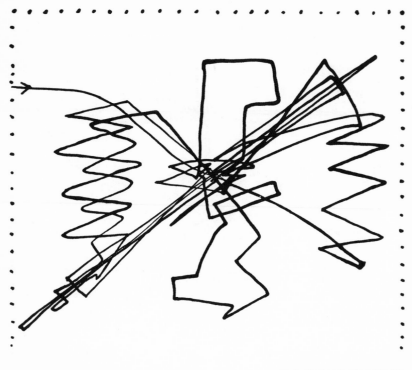

IMMEDIATE TRAGEDY

For the modern dancer who feels the need of placing her dance in a right relation to this age that is dominated by the machine and has been victor over space, there are not only all the old problems, but two that are essentially new. The first of these is how to make the human body, which is all the dancer has to work with, as sure as the machine, and yet keep it always as free as the spirit within, which keeps man from being a machine?

44

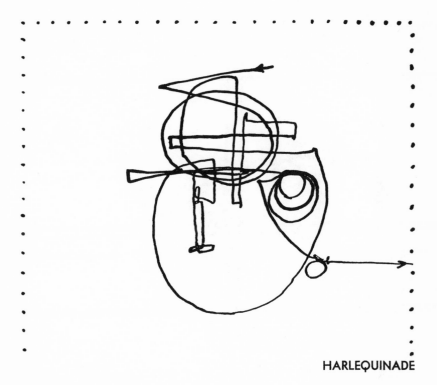

HARLEQUINADE

How, in other words, to make the body so adept, flexible and obedient that it will do completely and exactly whatever is demanded of it and so that it can express the intention of every movement through the clarity of the movement itself?

Perhaps Martha Graham, when she began, recognized this problem as the one that she must solve before all others; more likely---since she is not first of all an intellectual---she found as she worked, what an excellent medium of expression the human

45

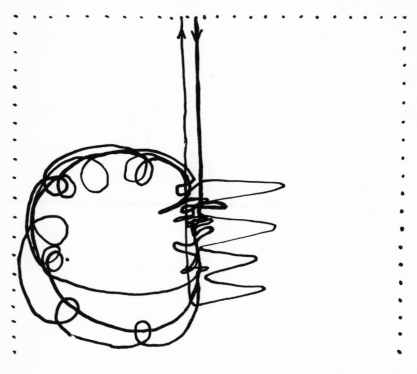

ACT OF PIETY

body is when you can master its potentialities, and so set herself sternly to that task. Certainly that is her first great contribution to the modern American dance: the body trained to obey the artist's will. That is quite a different thing from training the body in a difficult but limited convention, as in the ballet, or in a special and elaborate symbolism, as in the Oriental dance. The modern way leaves the artist and not the style always the master of an instrument as nearly as possible perfected for his use, and yet---from its human quality---an instrument never quite perfect or quite free, but always controlled by its relation to the earth from which it springs. This all good modern dance emphasizes by keeping the body in close contact with the earth, not merely making a pattern of steps on the floor, not only seeking release in elevation, but with every step somehow coming back with its full weight to the living earth as if still and always a part of it.

To have mastered so much would seem to be enough of an accomplishment, but it is not enough. It is only sharpening the tools of the trade. The dance as an art is far more demanding than that, and the dancer's second new problem, in the answer to which all creative modern dancers are still involved, is how, in the day of the radio and the airplane, to define and limit the scale of the space through which the dancer moves---how to relate this well-equipped body, excellently trained to expression, to the space through and within which it moves, so that the dances it creates shall seem vital and integrated. For, except in a purely personal or religious ritual, a dance is performed not only for the dancer but for those who watch the dance, and the selection and arrangement of movements must, if they are right, take a form which the watchers will respond to with satisfaction and recognize as true and beautiful. It is the sculptor's problem raised to the nth degree.

It is quite true for the dancer, as for other men, that one of the tests of genius is the ability to work within limits. But that test refers to the limits within the art itself. The dancer's limitation at the moment is outside the art and mechanical. Our stages are wide and shallow, and straight, horizontal lines are hampering and often meaningless in the modern dance. This bondage of space is one from which the dancer must be set free before the dance is free, before the second great problem is solved.

Up at Bennington on the open floor of the Armory---with the bondage of stage space removed---Arch Lauterer this summer followed the lines of some of Martha Graham's best-known dances and of the newest dance, "Immediate Tragedy". The sketches were made in half darkness and while Mr. Lauterer was watching the dance, without the opportunity to check his line against the dancer's movement. Yet even in this way, they make a portrait both of the dancer and of the dance that is clear and free and modern. They point the way ahead.

Y O U N G   1 9 3 2

Tennyson observed that of all things sculpture is one of the most difficult to describe. Dancing is even more so. We may, with writing talent, find some equivalent in words for a dance we write of. But this is a recreation of essence. It is not description. You could say, in fact, that the more exactly you describe such a dance composition the less you convey it to the reader. It might, however, be somewhat useful by another method.

49

When I first saw Miss Graham dance I had a feeling of insistent denial that I resented; too many things were cut away that life knows to be enchanting or profound. I thought I saw that this was a dancer who, having heard much of reaching the heavenly sphere, had brains enough to know that, while all art when it has arrived does indeed move within a heavenly sphere, it must, nevertheless, find first an earth to stand on. In sum, she knew that to look up at the stars you must have and use a head, eyes, neck, backbone and feet, plus the ground under you; it was not a mere matter of your feeling inside you that you were looking up at the stars, as if a feeling were anything people care about unless it achieves a form, a body in which it lives. There was, then, in Miss Graham's dancing this kind of stubborn elimination. It did show a sincere and genuine nature, but a nature not yet flowered in culture and freedom. There was also too great an absence of movement: the dancer's technique involved steps and positions, but the transition, which is the living element, was close to nil. From this early state all true at the time, to the artist and thus far right and moving on a human basis, Miss Graham has year by year progressed. You feel that her art has only just begun, and that one of the remarkable things about it is that this fact is even clearer to the artist than it is to you. There are, as every artist knows, a thousand ways to go forward by means of cheating surfaces void of inner solidity; the refusal of them is the first hallmark of an artist. From this most independent and self-imposed conviction of her present

50

stage of development, proceeds the freshness of Miss Graham's work. She knows that the first young stages of an artist have no freshness; they have only fresh feeling, or egotism or exhibitionism that is but partially expressed in form that is either casual or traditional or imitative. As the artist's work grows its freshness is present. Maturity alone brings it alive, into a complete life. Maturity implies not only the freshness and immediacy of feeling or idea---whatever you want to call it. It implies also that the technique to express it is safe, complete. When maturity is past, an artist may sometimes go on for no little while merely by remembering and repeating these already achieved forms, which, because of their rightness once, carry about them still something of their first desire and light.

It will be worth more to try and put down, rather than a report or attempted picture of Miss Graham's dance, some indication of what one can see is the process of her creation. Her dancing is pictorial, necessarily, since one understands it through the eyes. It is not pictorial in the sense of being representative, but pictorial as is an abstract painting or a pattern in design. She must begin, I should say, not with either a pictorial representational idea (some scene or personage) or with a dramatic idea: her first idea will be more like that of a designer of patterns, lines, angles, rugs, tiles, fabrics, what you will, or like the basic outlay of what will later be a painting. From this pattern or single form there will develop other forms; which in their turn may suggest an idea less visually abstract and more a subject,

51

more a literary or psychological meaning, and go on from there, perhaps, even to a title for the composition, "Incantation," say, or "Dolorosa" or "Dithyrambic."

Of "Primitive Mysteries" I can say that it is one of the few things I have ever seen in dancing where the idea, its origin, the source from which it grew, the development of its excitement and sanctity, give me a sense of baffled awe and surprise, the sense of wonder and defeat in its beautiful presence. By this I mean to imply a contrast with such a fine dance, for example, as Pavlova and Nijinsky in a bacchanal. Beautiful as that may have been, one could easily see how the idea might come from a vase painting, a bas relief, a flash of music. This predictability, so to speak, in no way lessened the excellence of that dance: I am only trying to express the other sense, of the wonder at creation and the feeling of an unimaginable origin and concentration. Miss Graham's dances have been so far both pictorial and dramatic, as music is, not as, for instance, a picture of Velasquez is, or a scene in a play.

There has been hitherto in her work an evasion of the dramatic, a concentration on the stark pattern for the design-idea of the composition. The benefits of this---for a period of time, that is---are manifest in the fine cleanness and purity of her dancing; we have the sense that, whatever may have been left out, nothing has entered a composition that has not grown into it organically.

We can make another interesting note on Miss Graham's

dancing. Certain reiterations are manifest, the return of a form, a tone, or rhythm. This seems to me a very wise tendency. The lack of reiteration is one of the things that send so much modern art off into nothing. There is not only the hypnotic effect of repetition and the satisfaction, as close as the pulse beat, of recurrence. A thing must return on itself as a part of its life process. The dance especially, involved so immediately with life, is gone as soon as it is finished, just as life is gone as soon as it ceases. Underlying all that is alive is the compulsion toward return. 1932

53

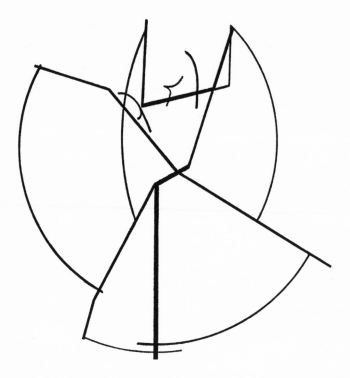

H A R G R A V E   1 9 3 7

Much has been written of the technique of Martha Graham.
Even the uninitiated can recognize at a glance that hers indeed
is an amazing equipment. But to the layman, recognition of this
technique is of as little help to an appreciation of her work as
reference to the "Twelve-sound structure" or "vertical

harmonics" of a Schoenberg would be to the uninitiated approaching modern music.

I may as well confess I find myself more interested in Martha Graham's work from the standpoint of the layman than from the point of view of the dance student, because I believe that her true importance lies in the projection of an emotional force which, while it may influence the dance form of a period, cannot be transmuted into a tangible enough substance to offer a credo to the dance movement of which it is a part. Contrary to such forms as the Diaghilev Ballet Russe, Graham's attack is directed basically toward the emotions rather than the eye; the receiving apparatus lies almost entirely in the *feeling* equipment of the spectator and not in rationalization.

Such projection of emotion cannot become part of a system of thought or teaching. It is by its specific nature part of that unique pathological function which is accurately spoken of as *genius*. At the risk of bringing down on my head the anathema of certain dance critics (and possibly of Miss Graham herself), I nevertheless would like to express the conviction that her particular form of dancing assumes its greatest importance by furnishing her with a medium of expression rather than by making any permanent contribution to ultimate trends. in the dance. Her perfect functioning in the form she chooses has a molding effect on the dance sphere of her time, naturally enough; but (also naturally enough) it could very well be a temporal functioning and remain fully as important. For just as she has created this

55

specific model of plasticity, she may ultimately break the mold (as she has done in the past) and fashion a new set of contours which would be equally serviceable to her unique gift.

As if in corroboration of this theory, Graham achieves some of her most startling moments by creating effects which are not essentially part of any dance form, in the accepted sense of the word, but rather instances of an ability to crystallize nebulous intensity into theatrical tangibilities; tangibilities which normally would seem to need the medium of painting or the written word to give them transmission. In the group of dances which she titles "Primitive Mysteries" she gives a spectacular demonstration of this ability, particularly in the "Crucifixus". During a considerable portion of this part or subdivision she stands immobile, transfixed in the center of the stage, her hands pressed tightly into the sides of her face. For a time all movement is left to her group while she resorts to projection through a sort of emotional incandescence which seems to have no plausible mode of propulsion other than a sheer inner vitality. And by means of this abnormal motionless projection she conveys to the receptive audience a definite emotional portrait of a crucifixion, free from any literary connotation, but nevertheless overwhelming in its flood of sorrow and ecstatic pain. Yet she makes no movement and she makes no sound.

Again, in "Frontier" (surely one of the most remarkable exhibits of the contemporary stage) she displays the phenomenon still further. Without a word, against black curtains, with no scenery but the suggestion of a gate and two abstract diverging lines, she summons up a complete sense of the American Western Plains couched in color, space and lineal horizon. She shades her eyes with her hands and looks across the stage and the boundaries of the theatre dissolve into frightening distance; standing small and female in all this space she has engendered, she brings an essence of strength and ecstasy, fear and power into play . .. and one is filled with pleasure at knowledge of the simple courage that lies potentially within humanity; a pioneer humanity that makes the lovely gesture of coping with the earth. With a curious quick shuffling movement of her feet, she makes her apparently motionless body move rapidly over the stage, cutting sizable geometric squares from its surface; and what seems to be a miracle has happened, for the squares are no longer cut from the floor but from measureless Western areas and the theatre is filled with a sense of speed and travel and wind; wind which sweeps vast untouched plains while she herself remains the focal point, transfigured with the vitality of possession. One need not be familiar with the dance idiom to understand what she is doing; all that is necessary is a receptive mind and the knowledge of Space: the experience of having, as an individual, *felt* Space oneself. For, Proust-like, she speaks to one's sense of recollection; she knows the truth that art can only articulate and broaden what one already knows, and wisely she keeps her approach abstract enough to let each one find his own response within himself.

57

Such achievement seems to be inexplicable in terms of natural phenomena; it seems rather to partake of black magic, to be compounded of some strange alchemy of the spirit whose source lies hidden in a dark inscrutable place. But this inscrutability, this curious esoterism, is perhaps the very quality which constitutes the sharp difference between talent and genius.

◆ ◆ ◆

Of all the words in language, "genius" is, I think, the most abused; it is thrown about with such unreasoning abandon that even people of discrimination apply it to almost any developed talent. Whereas, in reality, *genius* is a phenomenon which has appeared in the several centuries of mankind's history with disconcerting rarity. What it precisely *is*, of what it is constituted, offers a most complex and ponderable question. Is it an illness, a neurosis, a disease? Is it a kind of cosmically generated force which uses the human body as an agent of function, without atomically lessening the quantitative source; or is it the result of an inharmonious arrangement of neural organisms, finding escape from maladjustment and frustration in harmonious, prodigious creation? Such brains as Jung's and Adler's have struggled with the question, and they have risen from the combat, gasping for breath, sharpened by the exercise, but still without the final, definitive answer. Although the ultimate explanation lies hidden within the veiled future of the medical sciences, one thing seems certain: whatever genius is, it is *not* talent, even though it may bear some obscure relation to it. But even if we cannot explain genius, we can note with excitement that it is touched in all its instances with that esoteric quality which borders, in its prodigious, abnormal functioning, on the supernatural; a quality which seems to enable one to say that which is "unsayable", to make tangible that which is intangible, and to turn translucent that which is not translucent. . . .

The essence of that inner flux of the subconscious, for instance, which possesses some actor or actress so that he may sit motionless in a chair upon the stage and fill the theatre with the magic of wordless, elusive beauty, is utterly impervious to formulation or analysis. It is not a thing which can be acquired or achieved; it can, at best, only be fed and nourished so that it may increase, within its own potential stature, into full-flowered growth. Pauline Lord offers one example of this anomaly, I believe, in her adroit manipulation of the unspeakable nuances of attenuated inner emotion; Duse did, certainly; but one must wrack the brain to find other examples of it on the contemporary stage. While Graham usually demonstrates it in conjunction with movement, by itself it cannot in any literal sense be established categorically as pure dancing, for obviously it demonstrates itself in many instances completely apart from movement. Her extraordinary use of it probably bears more relationship to the art of acting than it does to the dance; but that is a moot question and, in the face of the rarity of Graham's gift, one, it seems to me, of sciolistic unimportance.

In acting a person may possess a great talent and develop that talent into the most highly polished skill which may well offer a credo or method for the student of acting to follow; because such skill and development, constructed as it is of tangibilities, can be subjected to careful analysis. Similarly, in ballet, one may establish a principle of teaching, for the instrument of transmission lies in tangible physical acts, i.e., arabesques, *entrechats, tour jetees*. . . . But the things which are most remarkable about Graham *cannot* be condensed into form. Give a dancer, no matter how proficient technically, all the outward contours, gestures, and movements of "Frontier" and you will have everything but the essence of the amazing thing which Graham herself does. The geometrical squares will be cut from so many feet of ground cloth and not from the rawness of earth, the shaded eye will make you aware of the nearby cyclorama instead of distant horizons, and the synthetically induced intensity is likely to produce merely the embarrassment of young hysterics. For Graham's intensity is an enormous thing which defies imitation and escapes the confines of pattern; she seems to generate and crystallize it into a form quite apart from herself; a form which springs from her body to exist freely on its own plane.

It is possible of course for her to transmit the physical design of her creations and their ideological content to other dancers. Her group is probably the best trained of any of the American dance groups and yet, in absorbing that which is teachable, they automatically prove the futility of that absorption. For example:

60

following the end of each section of "Primitive Mysteries" all the dancers turn, stand in silence for a moment and then, to a heavily accented beat, walk slowly from the stage. The co-ordination of the body, the placement of the foot, and the immutability of the tempo, all are nicely achieved by the group; but Graham brings something else into play and, as one *feels* it, one instinctively realizes that it alone is the all-important thing and that it bears no relation to technique. The difference lies simply in the fact that each member of the group seems to take the first step because it is timed to a beat, whereas Graham seems to step because the beat itself has forced her to move. One almost sees the beat drawn from the ground beneath her, like current from fused poles of fluidity; fluidity drawn slowly upward through feet and legs until the whole body becomes energized with potential movement; then, and then only, does she step, not because it is time, but because she inexorably *must*.

At her deliberate stimulation one feels the emotions she creates as entities in themselves. She talks in her own idiom of things which cannot be said and she enriches inner experience. She creates theatrical excitement with dances like the impudent "Imperial Gesture" and the poignant "Lamentation". And she makes of a simple thing like running, a joyous physical experience.

In painting and music and sculpture, such transparencies of the human spirit are capable of extension within the glass of time. But in dancing . . . these are ephemeral things, like dust

61

that blows with the wind. They are contained only within the instrument which creates them, and tragically they must of necessity perish with that instrument.

Perhaps therein lies a part of Graham's excitement.

S W E E N E Y   1 9 3 7

In the fields of art and literature there is little question but the
first third of the XXth century, when looked at in retrospect, will
be regarded as a period dominated by architecture and the dance
in a similar way to that in which music colored all the important
directives in art-expression and art-experience during the last
quarter of the XIXth century. And perhaps the influence of the

63

dance has been the more fundamental. That is to say, those phases of the dance which constituted a fresh, muscular assertion of clear-cut rhythmic pattern.

With the closing years of the XIXth century a condition began to be recognized which called for special consideration. About the beginning of the XVIIIth century, in all the arts, a greater rigidity in matters of minutiae had forced a break-up of the large forms and eventually destroyed the sense of the "main form". Previous to that time in the field of music a composition was seen primarily as a structure---certain main forms were filled with certain decorations. With the main forms stressed and a generous freedom allowed in the minor elements for improvisations and thematic variation, the musicians' constructive faculty was stimulated. But "notators gradually ceased to trust to, or expect intelligence on the part of the interpreter". The result was that the whole major structure of a piece of music became obscured; the incidental elements, the detail, showing on the score equally with the cardinal contentions of the composer.

In painting, between the opening of the XVIIIth and the close of the XIXth centuries, a similar decadence was taking place. To realize it one need only consider the growing emphasis on academic detail in one school, or the realistic minutiae of another and the minute particularization regarding light and color among the Impressionists. "Any work", as Ezra Pound put it twenty years ago in his *Pavannes and Divisions*, "is a compound of

64

freedom and order. It is perfectly obvious that art hangs between chaos on one side and mechanics on the other. A pedantic insistence on detail tends to drive out the 'major form'. A firm hold on the major form makes for freedom of detail. In painting, men intent on minutiae gradually lost the sense of form and form-combination. An attempt to restore this sense is branded as 'revolution' ".

And in literature we have the hardening of the late classical style in the XVIIIth century. * Then, the protest of a complete formal reaction among the extreme romantics leading to the machine-like technique and detailed, "scientific" naturalism of Zola and the objective, impassive perfection of the French Parnassians around Leconte de Lisle,---Huysmans' "sonorous hardware man".

The situation is clear. And the last quarter of the XIXth century already saw a conscious attempt to remedy it. In both literature and painting a turn was being undertaken from the realists' glorification of detail-for-its-own-sake and classicism's set forms, and frozen, encumbering ornament, toward a fresh realization of organic form. As early as the Great Exposition of London in 1851, the intelligent Occidental's confidence in

---

* For, by a "major form" is not intended a frozen convention of metronome expression but a flexible basis of expressional organization. Even during the "classical period" we read in Francois Couperin's *L'Art de Toucher le Clavecin* (1717): . . . "I find we confuse Time or Measure with what is called Cadence or Movement. Measure defines the quantity and quality of the beats; Cadence is properly the spirit, the soul that must be added. . . . Although these Preludes are written in measured time . . . those who will use these set Preludes must play them in an easy manner without binding themselves to strict time, unless I should have expressly marked it by the word 'measure' ".

progress, in the efficacy of his reasoning powers, and in the infallibility of science to arrive at truth, had begun to waiver. And in the face of this growing uncertainty in man's mind regarding the world about him and his relationship to it, he began to experience a profound need for the psychological reassurance of pattern and a living pattern in all about him and especially his expressions. At first this pattern was sought on a musical basis. And we see, as Walter Pater put it, in the latter quarter of the XIXth century, all arts approach the conditions of music. According to Paul Valery, "That movement which was baptized 'symbolism' is very simply summed up in the intention common to many families of poets to take up music as their ideal. The secret of the movement is nothing other than this". Painting with the "Synthetists"---Gauguin, Serusier and their associates ---was based primarily on "the arabesque", in Friederich Schlegel's words, "the simple musical swaying of the line itself, ---the oldest, the original form in which human imagination takes place".

And as long as there were still some remnants of the old human self-sufficiency of the Industrial period left, the reliance on a musical pattern was sufficient. But, by the opening of the XXth century, the last shred of this confidence seemed to have disappeared. And now a new fundament had to be found. For the younger generation the organization of expression along musical lines was not sufficiently basic. They felt that they must strip away the old superstructures in every field of expression in order

66

to uncover the foundations on which new and sound forms might be built. We see this attitude in the new formal interest in folk art and primitive expression of the early years of the century; again in the emphasis on "functional form" in architecture on one hand, and in the interest in psycho-analytic research on another. And with digging below the surface there came a new realization that beneath visual form lay a conceptual reconstruction of recollected motor experiences; that behind speech lay gesture; behind music, the dance; and that, beneath all, lay a rhythmic pattern which, emphasized in the specific means adopted, gave a new strength and sense of immediacy to expression.

In the field of architecture, as early as 1898, we find the Austrian, Adolf Loos, already writing against ornament * along similar lines to those of the "form follows function" attitude which the American Louis Sullivan had, in all probability, learned from his associate, Dankmar Adler, during their association in the later eighties and nineties. 1906 saw the earlier expressionist interest in negro sculpture turning to a more strictly plastic, analytico-structural approach. Before the war we have the austere cubist analyses and reconstruction of Picasso's 1913 period; between 1923 and 1926, the stark structures and chromatic counterpoint of Leger's most forceful period; and earlier, as well as since, Gabo's and Pevsner's constructions in

---

* "The lower the standard of a people, the more lavish are its ornaments. To find beauty in form instead of making it depend on ornament is the goal toward which humanity is aspiring"---*Ins Leere gesprochen* (1898).

metal and other materials. While in the dance we have a kindred return to formal bases in Martha Graham's sparing use of materials—her stripping of expression to the barest essentials, and, especially since 1930, in her interest in intensification through "percussive movement".

Finally a gradual reestablishment of "major forms" in the various fields of art has lead to a new conviction and validity of expression. But this is not sufficient. As a new form was necessary now a new philosophy of form---a new aesthetic---must be found. And any valid aesthetic, though it may be especially concerned with the arts, must be applicable to the whole range of human activities. To approach art the old aesthetic bases are no longer satisfactory. The old words have ceased to carry any live significance. As Professor Walter Gropius has recently pointed out, "The profound social revolution within the last generation, mainly caused by the inventions and development of the machine, has cut off the slow, genuine growth of creative art in all civilized countries. The succeeding gigantic struggle of coming to terms with the machine and getting it under control seems to have absorbed most of the vitality and creative power of those generations. The old conception of the basic unity of all art in its relation to life and the social strata of the community was therefore lost, and more and more replaced by that shallow esthetic 'art for art's sake' and the even more dangerous philosophy it sprang from: 'business is an end in itself'. The common attitude towards the arts turned consequently into a sentimental longing for historical forms by accepting aesthetic 'resentiment' and good taste as a substitute for creative art".

As a result of this break with the past, today new terms must be found for the discussion of aesthetic expression. A new common factor in expression must be uncovered. On this common factor we will then be able to construct a fresh approach. Martha Graham, with the contemporary poets, musicians, painters and architects, has been engaged in stripping away non-essentials and in emphasizing the "major form". The next step is the stripping of esthetic experience to its fundamentals. Beneath an esthetic experience we must look for a physiological experience. As a *raison d'etre* for pleasure from this physiological experience we will undoubtedly find an associable experience that satisfies some elementary physiological appetite or biological need.

To find this basis we must look back as far as possible to the earliest experienced sensations. And here the pattern, or rhythmic organization of parts, which we recognize in the arts today is possibly a lead. "Pleasure", as Ezra Pound has said in speaking of the eye, "is derivable not only from stroking or pushing the retina by lightwaves of various color but also by the impact of those waves in certain arranged tracts". And already before 1916 Jacques Dalcroze was teaching that "The common basis to the arts is more easily admitted than defined; but one important element in it---perhaps the only element that can be given a name---is rhythm. Rhythm of bodily movement, the dance, is the earliest form of artistic expression we know". And in looking for what may lie beneath the sensation of rhythm we read in Georg Groddeck: *

"The physiological conditions of pre-natal life when the child's impressions are in effect limited to the rhythmic beating of its mother's heart and its own, suffice to account for the deepest influence of music, an influence we find in the idea and word 'accord' ('accord' deriving from the Latin *cor* and undoubtedly signifying originally the harmonious beating of the hearts of the mother and child). And no doubt the swaying movement of the child within the mother's body helps to strengthen the development of a feeling for beat and rhythm."

Groddeck continues: "If one accepts the view that music has its origin in pre-natal experience, it is easy to proceed to a wider generalization, namely that music is the universal inheritance of mankind, for---and this is the core of my argument---music may be silent just as well as it may be served by sound; it may be heard, but it also may be seen; it is in essence beat and rhythm and so is bound up with man's innermost life. Man and the world which he creates for himself demand pulse and rhythm. . . . "

Perhaps the basic pattern is the heart beat.

And next to the wish to live lies the wish to remember.

---

* *Exploring the Unconscious.*

ANTHEIL 1937

Martha Graham is one of the greatest artists I know, and she is certainly in the very front line of American artists. But to understand Martha Graham one needs to understand a great variety of things; first and foremost, I think, one needs to understand America. But one also needs to understand the dancing of the immediate past as well as contemporary dancing to

71

understand just exactly how tremendous her revolution, how important her contribution.

None of us, surely, any longer believe that one can go straight to any work of art and appreciate it directly for its own values, be they aesthetic, intellectual, or sensuous. Picasso means nothing without the great line of revolutionary painters before him; the revolution of Strawinsky is not beautiful until one considers it alongside and after the revolution immediately preceding it---the revolution of Debussy. Unless all of these things are properly placed, we do not give the great artist his due---we merely place him in the same grab bag with a number of other (and perhaps more immediately attractive) artists.

Although Martha Graham is the very essence of America and its great background of plains, rivers, and western mountains, we cannot consider her without mentioning the names of European artists such as Pablo Picasso, Mary Wigman, Max Ernst, Gaudier-Brezka, Brancusi, and a host of others. The superimposition of these names upon the burning deserts of New Mexico is for me at least a very interesting equation; Martha Graham has not borrowed from them but she has grown up contemporaneously with them; it reminds me of the fact that the electric light bulb was invented in three different countries simultaneously.

There is no longer any doubt in my mind at least that mind-reading exists and that art movements are nothing but the expression of a common mass mental telepathy. Art movements begin to flow gradually but surely in one direction, like a great river. Sometime, in different eras, the river changes its directions, and rivers have even been known to stop and flow backwards. When this happens it is usually due to the machinations of man, or to an earthquake, usually the former. This was the case of the Chicago River. Critics can sometime make an art movement flow backwards, but in general art movements are very healthy things, completely logical, inevitable, and not to be dammed or suppressed unless the dammer, after a time, wishes to unleash upon himself a mighty flood.

Martha is an American expression of something completely contemporaneous that cannot nor will not be squelched. Martha may not be the balletmistress of the Philadelphia, New York, or San Francisco operas, but in Europe she most certainly would be. Or she would be adequately financed, as were the choreographers of the great European ballet troupes. But we, a young country, as graceless as the pioneer stock from which we sprang, treat our artists abominably. This is no secret, of course. We give every second-rate European a first-rate jump over the first-rate American; a thousand articles have been written about it and a million protests have been registered; why go into it?

But it is quite possible, indeed even quite probable, that enormous recognition and gorgeous background would not help Martha a whit. Barring financial independence, which is at all times desirable, I doubt very much whether Martha would wish or encourage a movement that would carry her into a Ballets

73

Russe theater sparkling with gay tunes rendered by a magnificent symphony orchestra. Hers is the art of subtraction rather than the art of addition. Although the toe-ballet calls itself classical, hers is the true modern classicism; modern toe ballet has added everything; Martha has taken everything away except the most prime essentials of dreams.

For Martha's art is a kind of American surrealism, a de-landscaping of a million American movements that have woven themselves into our American dream, a reclassification of these movements according to a *new* dream, (a dream of the future!) But her art is not simple. It is tremendously complex. People have called her art simple but I have an idea that Martha, like Dali, hates simplicity in all its forms. If her art has agricultural patience, it also has territorial ambivilance.

It is also quite possible that Martha, the maker of her dances, does not always know what they mean. Driven to giving them a title, she has often given her dances titles that would certainly tend to throw off the thoughtful observer. I rather regret this fact as the little hard titles which she uses makes one think of the inventions of inferior artists---men and women without imagination. But perhaps she avoids the true titles because she fears sensationalism in all its forms. Salvadore Dali, or Max Ernst, hardier men, are not afraid of anything, consequently their titles often hit nearer to the truth, which is the interior dream and spiritual essence.

I do not however believe that Martha is really afraid of

anything. I believe, rather, that Martha's gesture of hiding her magnificent work behind these nondescript titles is a gesture entirely true to her, a gesture as true as her reticent stage appearances. Because she herself (perhaps) does not understand her creation, this does not mean that it is any the less profound. Great art always was complex, coherent, and involuntary, and always escaped the most simple analysis of logical intuition.

In traveling over America this last year I have come to the conclusion that it is emphatically the domain of concrete irrationality. It has what Dali chooses to call the "most imperialist fury of precision." Precision, strange science growing grace, is the essence of Martha's creations. Certainly she has something which is almost hypnotic, a space consciousness that corresponds to the movements of the mesmeric hand; I have never seen another solo dancer who could hold his or her public spellbound for fifteen or twenty minutes of dancing. But in some strange way she is entirely American; one could never confuse her with any of the Europeans; I am sure that she will resent any "ism" references in this article, except American"ism". I cannot help that. I am not writing this article for Martha to like. No artist ever understands themselves. Other artists may not understand them either. But it is certain to every single one of us that Martha is one of those extraordinary *mediums* who read quickly and without knowing it present the mental telepathy of the race and concentrate its essence into the

75

movements of her body. In this she is almost unique. I know of only one *other* choreographer who does so---a man of the classic ballet at that.

Art and all its many movements have never been made by one man alone. But every so often one man comes along and does a tremendous "mental-telepathy" stunt. Such a jolt often puts art tremendously ahead.

When he does this we call him a "genius." I certainly believe that Martha is a genius.

It does not interest me particularly that she dances my music at times, nor how she dances it. It does not interest me whether or not she uses a classic technique or one which she has invented all by herself---all these things are ways and means and of tremendous importance only to the dancing world. I am of the music world. I understand things when I hear them, and that helps my eyes to understand. But I also understand things of the body, and of the muscles, for music is rhythm and comes out of the muscular flexs of a billion years as well as from the heart. The body, and its subleties speak to me. My heart misses a beat when her body hangs in the air and descends by a principle not known to ordinary man but by a principle only once known to the gods.

My heart keeps missing a great many beats when I look at the creations of Martha and her group. By this sign, even if by no other, I would know that she is a great artist.

She is in the greatest tradition of Strawinsky, Picasso,

Brancusi, Dali, Ernst, Cocteau, Breton, Aragon, Wigman, and herself! In their company my heart has missed a great many beats.

D A N Z   1 9 3 7

The Modern Dance is not a thing---it is a structural event. And as an event it exists only when performed. Furthermore, it exists even when it is not witnessed. Just as Modern Music still remains music although unheard and a Modern Abstract Painting is a Painting although it may never be seen by eyes other than those of its creator. A structural event is a "becoming." It has no

78

history. Its strength lies in its immediacy. And curiously, it cannot be recognized---it can only be cognized. Webster might have defined a structural event as: an organized cluster of dynamics coming into existence for a certain duration and developing organically to maturity only to eventually disappear ... and he could add: never to be repeated.

A structural event might become an apple or it might become a dance or music or an abstract painting. For instance, the object which we so casually name an apple is a structural event, but the moment it is named, it becomes a thing. Now although there are no two apples alike, we have no verbal mechanics by which we can define this distinction. To us, and rather superficially, an apple is just an apple and many apples are just many apples. And a dance is just a dance and Martha Graham's dance is just a dance. If you have seen her dance twice what you thought to be the same dance, you must realize that you have actually seen two separate and distinct dances. It would be impossible, even if she so desired, for Martha Graham to create two structural events exactly alike. A mother cannot give identical characteristics to two children---no, not even if they happened to be twins.

The Modern Dance of Martha Graham is not an objectification. And it can only be objectified by witnesses when it is misunderstood. It exists, as a cluster of dynamics organically maturing in that stillness we can only know as duration.

The Dance of Martha Graham is a structural event just as an apple is a structural event before it is called an apple. In the

79

Korzybski sense this is what happens: From the depths of her Neural Ego, which contains an indefinite number of organizational possibilities, Martha Graham projects a structure suitable for her esthetic desires. And to be fully cognized her dance must be witnessed at this point and not mentally carried over to become a thing, the story of a thing, nor even an object. A thing is not an object and an object is not an event. These are but stages in objectification. The impact of an event upon consciousness is powerful and direct, whereas the contact of a thing with thought is merely a sort of home coming. Because the thing as thing, originates solely in thought. A structural event is a neural projection---one could almost say---a nerve elongation. As such it lives as an organization in duration.

On the other hand, an art which concerns itself with things or the history of things cannot exist without witnesses because things live only in witnesses. It cannot be impersonalized. It is a last stage personal objectification. A Ballet, any sort of representational dance, burdened with the heavy hand of literature has no "becoming" but is a thing "become." And most significantly, it cannot be cognized, it can only be recognized. It is history re-presented---"Past" not "Present".

The term "Modern" obviously is quite misleading as it apparently includes every contemporary pot-boiler. I do not find that the term Modern as used in the arts has ever been clearly and conclusively defined. And yet, the definition is so simple and so fundamental that this should have been done a long time ago. In the first place, no person can be called modern ---that is, not in an art sense. Only a work of art can be *Modern*. And to be *Modern* means simply to be *Structural*.

What, then, is the difference between the art of today and the art of yesterday?

That can also be stated in very simple terms. The difference lies between representation and creation. Between dynamics and identifications. It is the difference between arranging some apples in agreeable sequence and making an apple.

But, some one shouts, who can make an apple? The answer is that no one can make an apple because there are no apples. As I have tried to show, apple is just a word objectified and nothing more. It is a rather crude label for a certain structural event which at that will not last long. It will eventually disappear never to return (Decay). The word, however, does not disappear, but stays on to be misapplied to another and another and another structural event. How blind is a word!

Modern art is not concerned with making any-*thing*. It is wholly bent on *Making*. The apple tree does not make apples. It merely *Makes*. We label the "make" an apple.

Martha Graham's dance is a structural event and of course we would have considerable difficulty if we tried to find a label for it, but, remember the man who first said apple, in all probability, had similar difficulty.

There are certain Bio-technic life forms. Crystals and spheres, cones, the plate, strip and rod, spirals and cubes. One finds all life expressed through them from the stars to the lowly snail. In the art of Martha Graham these forms, in their infinite variability, become real again---not as things are thought to be real---but as genuine creative events are real and actual.

Mathematics, Geometry and Numbers become neural and are projected as emotive patterns which live in space as well as in time---Nation-less, Race-less and name-less. Logic and reason become pure feeling. To witness such dancing is to be present in creative duration.

Martha Graham's dance is a structural event.

It is an Art-Act.

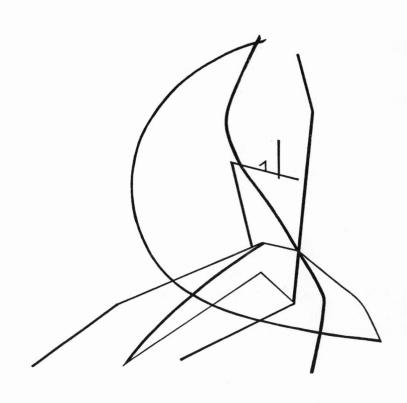

GRAHAM 1937

Throughout time dance has not changed in one essential function. The function of the dance is communication. The responsibility that dance fulfill its function belongs to us who are dancing today.

To understand dance for what it is, it is necessary we know from whence it comes and where it goes. It comes from the

83

depths of man's inner nature, the unconscious, where memory dwells. As such it inhabits the dancer. It goes into the experience of man, the spectator, awakening similar memories.

✦ ✦ ✦

Art is the evocation of man's inner nature. Through art, which finds its roots in man's unconscious---race memory---is the history and psyche of race brought into focus.

We are making a transition from 18th to 20th century thinking. A new vitality is possessing us. Certain depths of the intellect are being explored. Great art never ignores human values. Therein lies its roots. This is why forms change.

No art can live and pass untouched through such a vital period as we are now experiencing. Man is discovering himself as a world.

All action springs from necessity. This necessity is called by various names: inspiration, motivation, vision, genius. There is a difference of inspiration in the dance today.

Once we strove to imitate gods---we did god dances. Then we strove to become part of nature by representing natural forces in dance forms---winds---flowers---trees.

Dance was no longer performing its function of communication. By communication is not meant to tell a story or to project an idea, but to communicate experience by means of action and perceived by action. We were not speaking to that insight in man which would elevate him to a new strength through an heightened sense of awareness. Change had already taken place in man, was already in his life manifestations. While the arts do not create change, they register change.

This is the reason for the appearance of the modern dance. The departure of the dance from classical and romantic delineations was not an end in itself, but the means to an end. It was not done perversely to dramatize ugliness, or to strike at sacred tradition---to destroy from sheer inability to become proficient in the technical demands of a classical art. The old forms could not give voice to the more fully awakened man. They had to undergo metamorphosis---in some cases destruction, to serve as a medium for a time differently organized.

The modern dance, as we know it today, came after the World War. This period following the war, demanded forms vital enough for the reborn man to inhabit. Because of the revitalized consciousness came an alteration in movement---the medium of dance, as tone is medium. Out of this came a different use of the body as an instrument, as the violin is an intrument. Body is the basic instrument,intuitive, instinctive. As a result an entirely contemporary set of technics was evolved. While it had points of similarity with the old, that was because it was based on the innate co-ordination of the body which is timeless. With this enhanced language, and the more vitally organized instrument, the body, we are prepared for a deep, stirring creative communication.

All of this has nothing to do with propaganda as known and practiced. It only demands the dance be a moment of passionate,

85

completely disciplined action, that it communicate participation to the nerves, the skin, the structure of the spectator.

For this to be accomplished, however, it means that the communication be valid to the twentieth century man. There has been swift transition in this present recurrence of the modern dance. There was a revolt against the ornamented forms of impressionistic dancing. There came a period of great austerity. Movement was used carefully and significantly. Subject matter began to diverge---the dancer emerged from the realm of introspection. The dance began to record evolution in man's thinking. An impassioned dynamic technic was needed and gradually appeared. Dance accompaniment and costume were stripped to essentials. Music came to be written on the dance structure. It ceased to be the source of the emotional stimulus and was used as background. Music was used almost in the same sense that decor had been used in the older dance to bring the emotional content of the movement into focus for the spectator. As dance evolved into larger forms, music began to evolve also. The composer gained a greater strength and a more significant line from composing to meet the passionate requirements of the dance.

Then arose a danger. With music no longer acting in that capacity, what means to employ for focus---a focus suited to the eyes of today? Dance can remain for a time authentic, creative experience for the camparative few. There are those to whom focus is possible---because of their awareness and their response to the artist and his medium. But for the many the focus is not sharp enough to permit clear vision. At this point the responsibility rests with the dancer-choreographer. Now it seems necessary that the focus be made through sight.

While music for the dance is still transparent and exciting as an element, we still use the perennial black velvet curtain of another period as background. They were first used for the dance I believe by Isadora Duncan. She used them, from the same need we have today, to bring focus upon the dance, and she suceeded. But the dance today is another dance, brought into emergence by another orientation. Perhaps what Arch Lauterer calls "space man" will be as necessary to the dance of the future as the composer. All of life today is concerned with space problems, even political life. Space language is a language we understand. We receive so much of sensation through the eye.

It is understood without question that presentation can never take the place of the dance. It can only cover bad and unauthentic dancing as music was long able to do. But this evolved presentation will have nothing to do with dance decor in the older sense, which was basically a painting enlarged for the stage. At best it can only be an *accent* for the dance, evolved after the dance is finished. Dance decor can, I believe, serve as a means of enhancing movement and gesture to the point of revelation of content.

I refuse to admit that the dance has limitations that prevent its acceptance and understanding---or that the intrinsic purity of the art itself need be touched. The reality of the dance is its truth to our inner life. Therein lies its power to move and communicate experience. The reality of dance can be brought into focus---that is into the realm of human values---by simple, direct, objective means. We are a visually stimulated world today. The eye is not to be denied. Dance need not change---it has only to stand revealed.

88

THE PHOTOGRAPHS

EKSTASIS

SPECTRE 1914, FROM "CHRONICLE"

PORTRAIT WITH DYER "FRONTIER"

PRELUDE TO "TRANSITIONS"

SPECTRE 1914

PRAELUDIUM II

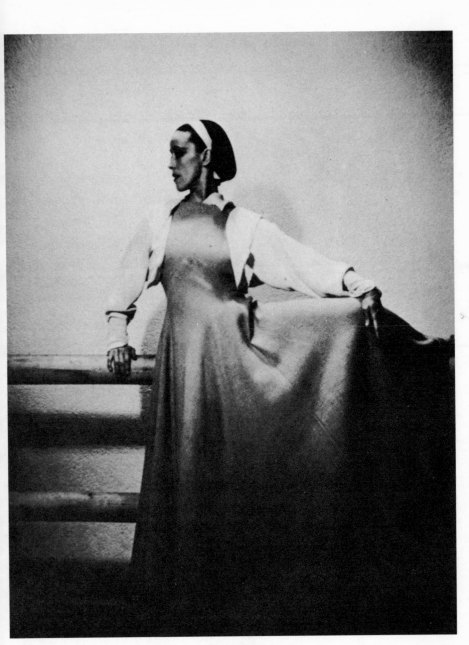

FRONTIER

FRONTIER, ACTION PHOTOGRAPH

LAMENTATION, ACTION PHOTOGRAPH

SARABANDE, ACTION PHOTOGRAPH

FRENETIC RHYTHM III, ACTION PHOTOGRAPH

PRAELUDIUM I

WAR, FROM SUITE "TRANSITIONS"

HYMN TO THE VIRGIN, FROM "PRIMITIVE MYSTERIES"

"CELEBRATION," GROUP DANCE

HILL SONG, FROM "HORIZONS"

ACT OF JUDGEMENT, FROM "AMERICAN PROVINCIALS"

REHEARSAL IN STUDIO

SARABANDE

PRIMITIVE CANTICLES

TRAGIC HOLIDAY, FROM "CHRONICLE"

PORTRAIT BY EDWARD BIBERMAN

CARLOS DYER "LAMENTATION"

LOUIS HORST BY SOICHI SUNAMI

L L O Y D   1 9 3 5

"Of the two arts that exist in time music has until recently had the grand monopoly. The dance has occupied the secondary place of interpreting music. In future the places may be reversed and music be relegated to the status of interpreting the dance. Even now, the symphony concert is largely a tonal museum." This startling statement was made by Louis Horst, the musician who for the past twenty years has worked solely in connection with the dance.

"Whoever heard of a lyre or a flute recital in ancient Greece? Music in ancient times was used only to attend dance or ceremony. In the classical period, as music came to the fore, the dance was pushed into the background. Now dance is coming into its own again and music as the whole show is paling into subdual."

"We know, generally speaking, that heretofore there have been three approaches to the use of music and dance. The old way was for a dancer to get an idea and then to look for a piece of music to fit it as a painter would paint a picture and then have to go buy a frame. The next advance is when the dancer has a mood or an idea and may have something written, but not absolutely independently, and then re-shapes it. That is the transitional period. We are now at a period where the dancer dominates---as she should---and has grown to be absolutely independent. She does the dance and creates the rhythm for it.

89

She then gets a composer to write the music upon the form she has created. Naturally, this will make the music secondary. The music is the frame to the picture. It is only an assistance to the dance but, that assistance is very important."

"Out of this situation a new musical profession is springing up---that of the composer-accompanist. New York is full of young musicians who are devoting all their attention to writing for the dance and accompanying dance performances."

Usually the composer sees the dance composition in its finished form before setting to work. Occasionally, the composer works with the choreographer. In the early days Mr. Horst not only wrote the music as the dance was being made, he made suggestions as to the movement itself, suitability of costume and lighting. It is doubtful if the modern dance in America would be where it is today were it not for his counsel and support.

He began, as did most of the important moderns, with Ruth St. Denis---when she came to San Francisco in 1915 and was suddenly in need of a new musical director. He arranged from the classics what he calls "hash scores" for dancing. Before that, he modestly avers, he was a hack musician, teaching, playing cafes and theatres. His instrument is the piano (he has studied violin). He was born in America, of German parentage. His father played trumpet in the San Francisco orchestra.

When the Denishawn company left for its Oriental tour in 1925, he went to Vienna to study composition. He found no "arty" atmosphere in Vienna, no hands over hearts bursting

Choreography by
Martha Graham.

Frontier

Music by
Louis Horst.

with inspiration, but straightforward, orderly, scientific procedure. This composing was a craft to be learned, and no nonsense. Seven months of it, without emotional trappings, equipped him for his subsequent plunge into the new dance movement. On his return to the United States, he played for Martha Graham at her first concert, in 1926. He worked with all the other significant young dancers of the day, and out of their need for more fitting music, began to compose for them.

Thus it is out of the dancers' need and not of his own compulsion that he composes. He is more interested in writing a score for a dancer than in writing something for himself. He has no desire to compose a separate musical composition that will stand alone. If it is too interesting musically, it obtrudes upon the dance. Music, for him, is the handmaid and not the mistress.

"Music for the dance cannot be judged apart from the dance for which it is written, because it is an integral part of it. I wonder what composers who have not heard the Mysteries would write---whether they would write academic music with development, bringing in different themes, counterpoint, and all the devices of theoretic composition? I took the flute and oboe and had them play in unison on the pentatonic scale throughout. In the interludes between each one of these phrases I used religious chords on the piano."

"Music can underscore or set off the dance, hold it in check, give it a certain boundary, for the body is the most dangerous of instruments and without the boundary of music and the authority of form, is likely to run riot in emotional expression. Motion is born of emotion (with the experienced dancer the process is sometimes reversed) and both must be kept under control. Then, too, the musical accompaniment provides aural assistance to the audience, giving emphasis to the movement, either by definitely underlining the rhythms or contrasting with counter-rhythms, with quiet passages of music to active passages of dance, or with energetic music against passive movement."

"The question is not how great a dance composer is, but what he does for the dance. The composer-accompanist must expect to sacrifice some of his identity as a musician when he writes or plays for the dance, although, just as the virtuoso accompanist to a singer, violinist, or other artist, is as important as a virtuoso performer, in his specialty, so a dance composer or accompanist is as important in his."

From the new conditions has developed a new course of study (as well as a new profession)---the composer-accompanist's course which Mr. Horst teaches at the Bennington Summer School of the Dance. He teaches in several schools and colleges, "composition in dance form." In this subject, the pupil is first taught musical form as a basis of dance form, the two arts being allied because of the time values inherent in each. When it comes to composition, the pupil is told to forget the rudiments and compose subjectively. So the knowledge of musical form will discipline without dominating the dance form. It will act subconsciously as a corrective to unleashed emotion, giving the thematic material of the dance phrasing and design that will enhance its content.

Louis Horst is Martha Graham's musical director. He has worked with her more than any of the other dancers, although he has in the past served all the important workers in the new field. He conducts for her a small orchestra of flute, clarinet, bass clarinet, trumpet and percussion. The strings, he says, are too luscious and romantic for the modern dance. In his own way he disposed of romanticism as he had previously disposed of emotionalism.

"The tone of the woodwinds seems to be more expressive of the character of the modern dance---the strings remind me of the court ballet. The combination of modern movement and diatonic scale melody produces a sentimental effect, besides, who writes in the diatonic scale today?"

Overuse of percussion (as the German dancers use it) is also too romantic, too Oriental. The German dance, Mr. Horst feels, is notably Oriental in root and trend. The brass supplies brilliance and vitality. The reed instruments give primitive coloring.

In the beginning of the modern movement in America, the use of percussion was a rebound from lyricism. The dancers had to go back to go ahead. They went back to the primitive in music and movement, to get rid of the soft, flowing things they had learned. They had revolted against ballet, against the Denishawn technique (a kind of barefoot, plastic ballet) but that is all they had done. They were at first inarticulate or inclined to give way

94

to emotional self-expression. To overcome this, they went through a period of sparseness, began with almost static dances. Gradually, as they discovered what the body could do, they freed themselves from the past, freed the dance from music as an absolute necessity. There was a period of silent dancing. Then they re-discovered music as a complement to movement and from this has arisen music for the dance as functional music. In this functional capacity, music for the dance has become more concentrated, more simple and direct.

"We are living in a transitional age---in politics, in the arts. We are moving forward, I hope, but the destination is still unknown. The artist is always a radical. If he is an artist he is progressive and if he is progressive he must break with tradition. All great art contains an element of social criticism, for it expresses the life of its time."

AFFIRMATIONS 1926-37

These statements have been made in interviews to the press, beginning with the year of my first independent recital in New York, 1926. They are presented as the record of one person's thinking during those years when the dance was coming of age in this country. A clear accent has been placed upon the consciousness of country. This was temporary but inevitable isolation necessary to find something akin to a folk condition of truth from which to begin. A necessary part of development was that we become aware of the ground on which we find ourselves, from which we have been bred physically and psychically. Once this narrow but firm base was established emergence could follow. From the ensuing relationships and the sense of responsibility so engendered, a deeper, richer art is arising, a communication, we hope, not only to one country, but by its innate vitality and truth, to all men.

Martha Graham 1937

◆ ◆ ◆

The gesture is the thing truly expressive of the individual---as we think, so we will act. 1926

◆ ◆ ◆

No animal ever has an ugly body until it is domesticated. It is the same with the human body. Civilization has made it impossible and undesirable for us to lead the rugged, hardy lives of our ancestors, but in the place of physical adventure,

96

which kept them alert, alive to the very finger-tips, we have a hundred-fold more mental adventures, which serve the same purpose of quickening our pulses and vitalizing our energies. To those who can become as open-minded as children the dance has a tremendous power; it is a spiritual touchstone.   1926

✦ ✦ ✦

Out of emotion comes form. We have form in music as the reflection of the composer's emotion. There is a corresponding form of movement, a dynamic relation between sound and motion. One can build up a crescendo either with a succession of sounds or with a succession of movements.   1927

✦ ✦ ✦

Any great art is the condensation of a strong feeling, a perfectly conscious thing.   1927

✦ ✦ ✦

Virile gestures are evocative of the only true beauty. Ugliness may be actually beautiful if it cries out with the voice of power.

✦ ✦ ✦   1928

Like the modern painters and architects, we have stripped our medium of decorative unessentials. Just as fancy trimmings are no longer seen on buildings, so dancing is no longer padded. It is not "pretty" but it is much more real.   1930

✦ ✦ ✦

Interest from America in the dance as an art is new---even to dancers themselves, fettered as they have been to things European. Recognition of the place the dance is destined to hold has been slow---but to a few it is already a peculiarly great force that is gradually assuming a form.

Granted that rhythm be the sum total of one's experience, then the dance form of America will of necessity differ greatly from that of any other country. So far the dance derived or transplanted has retarded our creative growth, in spite of the fact that there are thousands of ardent dance pupils in this country. It is not to establish *something American* that we are striving, but to create a form and expression that will have for us integrity and creative force.

As to form, which is the heart, there is beginning to be manifest an economy of gesture in the dance, an intensity and integrity of mood, a simplified external means, and above all a concentration on "the Stuff" of the dance, which is significant movement. Through its dancers so brilliantly springing to life and talent throughout the country will come the great mass drama that is the American Dance.   1931

✦ ✦ ✦

It is with the manifestation of an old art in a land newly growing aware that we should be concerned.

Dance in its varied forms and styles is directly affected by the country in which it manifests itself, but the physical principles of great dancing remain inherently the same. Although the manner of dancing may change so radically as to seem to affect these basic principles, the body, itself, which is the dancer's medium, is eternally subject to certain laws of rhythm definitely its own. Manner, however, is born of the climatic, social and religious conditions of the land in which the dance finds itself. This is the reason why a dance form, whether it be Spanish, Russian, Oriental, or even modern European, when transplanted or grafted on a completely alien culture loses its creative energy and becomes decadent or, at best, merely decorative. Any dance, however formal and stylized its manifestation, which does not stem from life itself will become decadent.

It is not possible for one people to understand another people entirely, or to feel with the soul of another. How then is it possible to adopt a dance from which is the revelation of a people's soul? Movement is the one speech which cannot lie. In movement all that is false, or too obviously learned, becomes glaringly apparent. This is important in considering the modern dance, for it is with movement, rather than with steps, that it is concerned.

America's great gift to the arts is rhythm: rich, full, unabashed, virile. Our two forms of indigenous dance, the Negro and the Indian, are as dramatically contrasted rhythmically as the land in which they root. The Negro dance is a dance toward freedom, a dance to forgetfulness, often Dionysiac in its abandon and the raw splendor of its rhythm---it is a rhythm of disintegration. The Indian dance, however, is not for freedom, or forgetfulness, or escape, but for awareness of life, complete relationship with that world in which he finds himself; it is a dance for power, a rhythm of integration.

99

These are primitive sources which, though they may be basically foreign to us, are, nevertheless, akin to the forces which are at work in our life. For we, as a nation, are primitive also---primitive in the sense that we are forming a new culture. We are weaving a new fabric, and while it is true that we are weaving it from the threads of many old cultures, the whole cloth will be entirely indigenous. The dancers of America may be Jewish and Spanish and Russian and Oriental, as well as Indian and Negro. Their dancing will contain a heritage from all other nations, but it will be transfigured by the rhythm, and dominated by the psyche of this new land. Instead of one school of technique ever becoming known as the American dance, a certain quality of movement will come to be recognized as American.

It has been said that the dance today is the unspanked baby of the American theatre. Most certainly it is the one lusty voice on the American stage. Many hear its voice as a prophecy of the possibility of a theatre of the future. History shows that the great theatre of the world, whether in Greece or the Orient, had its roots in the dance, and that the theatre of any culture is only as great as its dance. Why should not all those so deeply concerned with the modern drama see that it is not possible for the order of progress to be different?

The modern American dance is characterized, like the true dance of any period of world history, by a simplicity of idea, an economy of means, a focus directly upon movement, and

100

behind and above and around all, an awareness, a direct relationship to the blood flow of the time and country that nourishes it. To have an American dance we must take these characteristics as a starting point, then from a cognizance of old forms we shall build a new order.   1932

+ + +

One has to become what one is. Since the dance form is governed by social conditions, so the American rhythm is sharp and angular, stripped of unessentials. It is something related only to itself, not laid on, but of a piece with that spirit which was willing to face a pioneer country.   1933

+ + +

Artistry lies in restraint as much as in expression.

The dance today does not express a machine.

How can a man be a machine or imitate a machine?

There has been a change of tempo brought about by the machine. We can only express this tempo.   1934

+ + +

By balance I do not mean just the ability to hold one's balance, but rather your relationship to the space around you.

The most important thing for you as a dancer is your posture. Grace in dancers is not just a decorative thing.

Grace is your relationship to the world, your attitude to the people with whom and for whom you are dancing.

Grace means your relationship to the stage and the space around you---the beauty your freedom, your discipline, your

101

concentration and your complete awareness have brought you.

If you rely upon mood you will soon come to the point where that mood is gone or cannot be recalled at the particular time you need it.

If you have no form, after a certain length of time you become inarticulate.

Your training only gives you freedom.

The Modern Dance is couched in the rhythm of our time; it is urban and not pastoral.

The ideal of technique is the absence of strain; it is the rhythmic building of the body to a perfect form.

It is not important that you should know what a dance means. It is only important that you should be stirred.

If you can write the story of your dance, it is a literary thing but not dancing.   1934

♦   ♦   ♦

Nothing seems to be more dangerous than the notion that the dancer is not a hard worker and that the dance is effeminate. The dancer is, as all artists must be, one who works constantly with his material. The dance must be strong. If people would permit themselves to be moved, the dance would be a powerful influence. I would rather a thousand times have a specific antagonism than a cold indifference. In the former, at least, there is a presence of life---something to work against. Apathy is like a fog.   1935

♦   ♦   ♦

My dancing is just dancing. It is not an attempt to interpret life in a literary sense. It is the affirmation of life through movement. Its only aim is to impart the sensation of living, to energize the spectator into keener awareness of the vigor, of the mystery, the humor, the variety and the wonder of life; to send the spectator away with a fuller sense of his own potentialities and the power of realizing them, whatever the medium of his activity.   1935

◆ ◆ ◆

This is a time of action, not re-action. The dance is action, not attitude, not an interpretation. There is a change in the artist's attitude toward his material. The modern dancer does not look upon it as an escape, but finds it exciting. There is a miracle in yourself. No dance can be transplanted from one nation to another and retain its purity and integrity. . . . The history of the dance is the social history of the world.   1935

◆ ◆ ◆

It was right for Bernhardt to be glamorous; hers was an attitude toward life that belonged to her period.

I have always fought against any dramatization of my peculiarities or my personality. If you attitudinize or dramatize yourself, your sense of touch for new things is gone. You begin living on your own past. Talent or personal power, whatever it is, can turn and destroy you if you misuse it in any way.

The dance is not a literary art and is not given to words---it is something you do. There is danger in rationalizing about it too much.

103

Sports take a different set of muscles, and the dancer must not destroy his muscular memory, as it is not with his mind but with his body that he remembers.

The exponent of modern dancing has to fight two things. One is the belief that it simply means self-expression and the other that no technic is required. The dance has two sides---one is the science of movement, the technique which is a cold exact science and has to be learned very carefully---and the other is the distortion of those principles, the use of that technique impelled by an emotion.

The modern dancer uses costume as an integral part of the dance. There is always some reason why a dance should be in a certain color or a dress cut in a certain way. It comes out of the dance itself. Isadora Duncan used the Greek robe simply because it gave her the greatest freedom, but her dance was not Greek and she never intended it to be. However she was a Greek in her attitude toward life.

Costumes for the modern dance are very different from ballet costumes; they have grown out of the modern dancer's attitude toward movement. The costume has to be designed around the physical aspect of the dance.   1935

✦ ✦ ✦

Movement in the modern dance is the product not of invention but of discovery---discovery of what the body will do, and what it can do in the expression of emotion.   1935

✦ ✦ ✦

To the American dancer I say "Know your country". When its vitality, its freshness, its exuberance, its overabundance of youth and vigor, its contrasts of plenitude and barrenness are made manifest in movement on the stage, we begin to see the American dance.

When we speak of this country, we speak of a vast concept whose infinite facets cannot all be seen. But in spite of this immensity let us find the fundamentals of which we are all a part. Let us examine for a moment a striking difference in the Continent's and our own reaction to an important factor in modern times---the machine. Talk to the Continental, talk to the American of the machines' part in the tempo of modern life. The reactions are unmistakably characteristic.

To the European the machine is still a matter of wonder and excessive sentimentality. Some sort of machine dance is a staple to every European dance repertory. But to the American sentimentality for the machine is alien. The machine is a natural phenomena of life.

An American dance is not a series of steps. It is infinitely more. It is a characteristic time beat, a different speed, an accent, sharp, clear, staccato.   1936

✦ ✦ ✦

It is a mistake to believe that modern dancing is something unrelated to anything that has gone before. The dance is a universal art, certain aspects of which, basic position in particular, will be found all over the world. There can be no dancing of value without a foundation in technique and those today who are of most harm to the dance are those who practise ugliness for its own sake, as a form of personalized self-expression, without any ideas to give their work value. It is only by knowing the rules that it becomes possible to break and change them.

✦　✦　✦　　　　　1936

It takes ten years to build a dancer. The body must be tempered by hard, definite technique---the science of dance movement---and the mind enriched by experience. Both must be ripened to maturity before the dancer has a message he can convey effectually. A part of this maturity is muscular memory. It has nothing to do with so-called natural dancing or improvisation.　　　　　1936

✦　✦　✦

To me what I am doing is natural. It fits me as my skin fits me. I feel it is the natural beat of life today. Modern dancing requires the spectators' participation---the greatest theatre sense the audience can muster. They must allow themselves to be reached by economy, simplicity and necessity of line rather than by intricacy of detail or story values. But if you want to be soothed, entertained and lulled into a false sense of security, the modern dance is not for you.　　　　　1936

✦　✦　✦

Our creative dance has too often suffered because of our unwillingness to dig deep into our own experience. The dance can be and must be a powerful influence. Sometimes the audience reaction will be cold antagonism, sometimes unbelievable response. In either case the American dancer owes a duty to the American audience. We must look to America to bring forth an art as powerful as the country itself. We look to the dance to evoke and offer life.   1936

✦ ✦ ✦

As we begin to take more and more honor in the interpretation of the American scene, our dance takes deeper and deeper root. America does not concern itself now with impressionism. The psychology of the land is to be found in its movement.   1936

✦ ✦ ✦

No artist is ahead of his time. He *is* his time: it is just that others are behind the time.   1936

✦ ✦ ✦

In the early days of the dance renaissance in America a slowly rising arm signified growing corn or flowers; a downward fluttering of the fingers perhaps suggested rain. Why should an arm try to be corn; why should a hand try to be rain? Think of what a wonderful thing the hand is, and what vast potentialities of movement it has as a hand and not as a poor imitation of something else.

Movement comes from the body itself; not the movement of the body trying to adapt itself to a foreign element.   1936

✦ ✦ ✦

Dancing is a very living art. It is essentially of the moment, although a very old art. A dancer's art is lived while he is

107

dancing. Nothing is left of his art except the pictures and the memories---when his dancing days are over. What he has to contribute to the sum total of human experience must be done through the dance. It cannot be transmitted at any other time, in any other way. 1936

✦ ✦ ✦

I allow the form of the dance to give me back the certain emotional quality which goes with it. I do not put myself consciously into that mood before the dance. I strive at all times to let the thing happen to me. I remain as free as possible from any forced or extraneous prompting. But I must be very sure of all my movements. If my hand goes in one place one day it must go exactly the same place the next day. If in "Imperial Gesture" I lifted my skirt with two fingers in one performance, I must use the same two fingers in all succeeding performances. There is no varying of pattern. The pattern of the dance is as formal as the music. One remembers such movements with one's body muscularly. The thing has gone so deep within one that it is hard to say how one remembers.

I could not say what passes through my mind when dancing on the stage. I only know that then, extremely conscious of the audience, hypersensitive to sound and whisper, I feel my highest point of integration, if I have done my practising---if not, I am nervous, struggling, tense. 1936

✦ ✦ ✦

The ear should be in a straight line with the shoulder and the pelvis bone. That brings the head back, the diaphragm in. It shows the back of the head like a child's, and that is the effect it is supposed to give---like a child full of wonder and excitement.

◆ ◆ ◆ 1936

A dancer on the stage should be in command of all things physical. His work will become more clear and precise as his body becomes more certain and flexible. His performance should have an exact logic. The difference between the artist and the non-artist is not a greater capacity for feeling. The secret is that the artist can objectify, can make apparent the feelings we all have. 1936

◆ ◆ ◆

The modern dance of the present time began in America, strangely enough, particularly on the West Coast with Isadora Duncan and Ruth St. Denis. Both of these dancers had reached world recognition in their modern expression before the dance began as a modern movement in Germany. Both Isadora Duncan and Ruth St. Denis danced in Germany before the name of von Laban was known. While the trend did not originate in Germany, but in America through the two dancers who had influenced the entire world of dancing, there was a strong German school under von Laban and Mary Wigman in post-war Germany. The dance of the world has been enriched first by the initial American contribution, second by the Diaghilev Ballet, under Fokine, then by the German under von Laban and Wigman, and at the present time by the efforts of the American dancers. 1936

109

◆ ◆ ◆

Life does not have to be interpreted, and the dance is life. It has to be experienced, not taken apart and dissected. Dances affect the body, not just the mind. Dance is not a mirror, but a participation, a voicing of the hidden but common emotions.

◆ ◆ ◆   1937

The last fifty years brought a different vibration through inventions of telephones, radios, television. What has happened to artificial things has happened to the body. The movements are essentially the same, but the timing is different.

There is a necessity for movement when words are not adequate.

The basis of all dancing is something deep within you.

1937

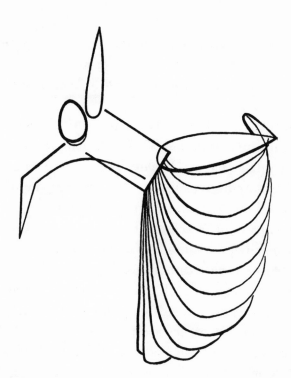

SARGEANT 1937

Martha Graham was born in Pittsburgh, Pa., the daughter of Dr. George Graham, a specialist in nervous diseases, who boasted a line of some ten generations of New England and New York Dutch ancestry. On her mother's side, she is a tenth direct descendant of Miles Standish. Her background gives out no exceptional clue. When she was eight the family moved to Santa Barbara, California, where in 1916 she came under the influence of Ruth St. Denis. She studied with her a short time, until bowing to parental pressure, she was forced to complete her schooling. In 1919 she returned to become a member of the Denishawn group.

Her debut as a professional occurred in 1920, when she made a six months' tour with Ted Shawn, dancing the leading girl's part in the Aztec ballet "Xochitl". She stayed with the Denishawn Company for four years, one tour taking her to London.

In 1923, John Murray Anderson saw her dance in the Denishawn Company in New York City and engaged her for the Greenwich Village Follies, in which she appeared for two seasons. She performed three dances, one Oriental, one Moorish, and one with a large veil, all in the Denishawn tradition. Realizing the inability to continue this tradition, and feeling she must find herself as a dancer, she accepted a position in Rochester to teach. Rueben Mamoulian recommended her to the board of the Eastman School of the Theatre as a dance instructor.

It was there she began to work seriously from within herself for the first time. It was also the first time she had worked with a group and here she began experimenting.

In 1926 she gave her first independent recital . . . at the Forty-eighth Street Theatre loaned to her by Al Jones, who had produced the Greenwich Follies. The recital was unsponsored. John Murray Anderson bought the first tickets to that performance.

It was from Denishawn she inherited the collaboration of the

112

pianist and the composer, Louis Horst, an invaluable critic and an important influence in her later work.

From her first recital in New York in the spring of 1926 it was apparent that a new approach was being evolved. Among a group of more theatrical conceptions (which included even at this late date one or two Oriental and Spanish items left over from Denishawn days), three dances showed the economy of means, the independence of the pantomimic and the absence of "interpretative" elements which were to characterize her later work. They were *Danse Languide, Désir* and the Gnossiennes suite which included the well known *Tanagra*. The press was mildly cordial, and---important---the box office paid expenses. The season of 1926-7 saw two New York recitals and the appearance of the *Baal-Shem* suite to music by Ernest Bloch. The second movement of this suite, *Contrition,* was important as being the forerunner of the later *Lamentation*. The following season closed her Scriabine period with three *Poems,* and a really revolutionary note made itself apparent for the first time in *Revolt* (Honegger) and in the satire *Tanzstuck* (Hindemith). Contemporary musical idioms were beginning to be felt as appropriate backgrounds for her works. The trend of protest which had been started in *Revolt* was continued at a second recital later in the season with *Poems of 1917* (Ornstein) and the two dances *Steerage* and *Strike*. At the same recital a precedent was set with the *Fragments,* to which Louis Horst had composed music after the creation of the dance itself.

113

Following an appearance in the Neighborhood Playhouse productions of Debussy's *Nauges et Fetes* and Bloch's *Israel* with the Cleveland Orchestra during the season 1927-8, she gave her sixth and seventh New York recitals. Her distinctive uses of mass group movements showed themselves this year in *Sketches from the People* and above all in the impressive *Heretic*, while her lighter satiric style continued in *Four Insincerities* (Prokofieff) and *Rustica* (Poulenc). In 1929-30 the Dance Repertory Theatre was organized and three recitals were given under its auspices. This year witnessed the creation of two dances which became more or less the standard parts of her subsequent repertoire: *Lamentation* (Kodaly) and *Harlequinade* (Toch). It also saw Miss Graham's only venture into the realm of unaccompanied dance in the soon abandoned *Project for a Divine Comedy*. This season was the close of a period of experimentation in styles and methods. Maturity was to follow. Meanwhile there had been an appearance with the Philadelphia Orchestra as the Elue in Stravinsky's *Sacre du Printemps* under Massine's direction, and a role in the Neighborhood Playhouse production of Loeffler's *Pagan Poem*.

In the fall of 1930 she visited the Indian country of New Mexico. A strong feeling for the ritualistic which had always been present in her approach received fresh impetus from the vast sage-brush deserts and the simple dark-skinned race of artists that inhabits them. A new mysticism crystallized, and was to furnish her future work with a central core. It was not as many have supposed, a Christian mysticism. Its roots lay rather in nature worship, belief in the wisdom of those who live close to the soil, faith in the perpetuation of something that is basically of this hemisphere---the "American rhythm" it has been called ---something at any rate, which is neither religious in the established sense, racial, nor national, but which is specific in culture.

The "primitive" series started during the following winter, with the *Primitive Canticles* (Villa-Lobos) and the *Primitive Mysteries* (Horst). This season also saw the first performance of the Reigger *Bacchanale,* remarkable for group virtuosity, and the *Rhapsodics* out of which grew later the *Dithryambic.* The following season, that of 1931-32, she danced to her first sold-out house, presenting *Dithryambic* (probably her most ambitious and completely integrated solo composition), and adding three new works to the primitive series: *Incantation* (Villa-Lobos), *Dolorosa* (Villa-Lobos) and the large cycle *Ceremonials* (Engel). In March 1932 she received the Guggenheim fellowship for a Summer of study in Mexico.

At the opening of the Radio City Music Hall in December of the same year the *Choric Dance for an Antique Tragedy* was presented, later to be incorporated as the third movement of the cycle *Tragic Patterns.* Another theatrical venture of the season was the staging of the movement for Katherine Cornell's production of *Lucrece* which opened in January 1933. Still another was the choreography of six miracle plays produced by Natalie Hammond at the Guild Theatre. A season richer in ventures of this sort than in pure dance productions closed with a spring recital which nevertheless included *Ekstasis* (Engel) and *Tragic Patterns* (Horst).

The beginning of the New York season in November 1934, saw an important addition to her repertoire and the beginning of a definite trend in her development as an American dancer. *American Provincials,* comprised of two parts, the *Act of Piety* and the *Act of Judgment,* was performed for the first time. The same evening saw the first appearance of *Dance in Four Parts* to the music of 25 short preludes by George Antheil. This same month she composed and directed the dances for Katherine Cornell's production of *Romeo and Juliet.*

The first concert of 1935 in February, marked the return of a new lyricism to both the solo and group dances. Paul Nordhoff's lyric *Praeludium* was first performed with another important lyric composition for the group, *Course* (Antheil). In April, that year, was made the most important contribution to her solo repertoire, *Frontier.* This dance was to become almost a personal seal. Also in that spring she directed the movement for Archibald Macleish's verse-play, *Panic.*

The summer of 1935 saw the first workshop performances of the Bennington School of the Dance at Bennington, Vermont. On August 14-15, Miss Graham presented *Panorama* (Norman Lloyd), a large composition for an augmented group of thirty-six. It was her first work of such extended form. The year, 1935,

116

also saw the appearance of *Imperial Gesture*, marking a recurrence of dances, socially inspired.

In March, 1936, came *Horizons* (Horst), a large group composition, using for the first time moving objects on the stage, Mobiles by Alexander Calder, as an attempted visual prelude to the dance. This was an experiment and proved unsuccessful. In December, of the same year, was given *Chronicle* (Riegger); it was an extended composition, anti-war in character, done in suite form for group and solo figure.

The summer of 1937, at Bennington, witnessed an evolvement of style in the new dance *Immediate Tragedy*, with music by Henry Cowell. This and a new opening dance to the music of Norman Lloyd marks the career of Martha Graham to date.

117

NEW YORK CONCERTS & REPERTOIRE

1st New York Concert---April 18, 1926. 48th Street Theatre.

*DANCE LANGUIDE *(Scriabin)*---for a group of three.
*DESIR *(Scriabin)*---solo.
*DEUX VALSES SENTIMENTALES *(Ravel)*---solo.
*TANAGRA *(Satie)*---solo.

118

2nd New York Concert—Nov. 28, 1926. Klaw Theatre.

*CONTRITION *(Bloch)*---solo.

3rd New York Concert—Feb. 27, 1927. Guild Theatre.

*LA CANCION *(Defosse)*---solo.

4th New York Concert—Oct. 16, 1927. Little Theatre.

*REVOLT *(Honegger)*---solo.
*FRAGILITE *(Scriabin)*---solo.

**5th New York Concert—Feb. 12, 1928.
Civic Repertory Theatre.**

6th New York Concert—April 22, 1928. Little Theatre.

*IMMIGRANT---*a.* STEERAGE; *b.* STRIKE *(Slavenski)*---solo.
*POEMS OF 1917---*a.* SONG BEHIND THE LINES; *b.* DANCE
OF DEATH *(Ornstein)*---solo.
*FRAGMENTS---*a.* TRAGEDY; *b.* COMEDY *(Horst)*---solo.

7th New York Concert—Jan. 20, 1929. Booth Theatre.

*DANCE *(Honegger)*---solo.
*FOUR INSINCERITIES---*a.* PETULENCE; *b.* REMORSE;
c. POLITENESS; *d.* VIVACITY *(Prokofieff)*---solo.

8th New York Concert—Mar. 3, 1929. Booth Theatre.

*ADOLESCENCE *(Hindemith)*---solo.
*UNBALANCED *(Harsanyi)*---solo.

119

9th New York Concert---April 14, 1929 (Debut of the Group). Booth Theatre.

*VISION OF THE APOCALYPSE *(Reutter)*---group.
*RUSTICA *(Poulenc)*---group.
*SKETCHES FROM THE PEOPLE *(Krein)*---group.
*HERETIC *(Breton song)*---group.

10th and 11th New York Concerts---Jan. 8 and 11, 1930. First Dance Repertory Theatre Season. Maxine Elliott Theatre.

*LAMENTATION *(Kodaly)*---solo.
*HARLEQUINADE---*a*. PESSIMIST; *b*. OPTIMIST *(Toch)*---solo.
*A PROJECT IN MOVEMENT FOR A DIVINE COMEDY (first and only dance completely without music)---group.

12th and 13th New York Concerts---Feb. 2 and 6, 1931. Second Season of Dance Repertory Theatre. Craig Theatre.

*PRIMITIVE CANTICLES---*a*. AVE; *b*. SALVE *(Villa-Lobos)*--- solo.
*PRIMITIVE MYSTERIES---*a*. HYMN TO THE VIRGIN; *b*. CRUCIFIXUS; *c*. HOSANNA *(Horst)*---group.
*RHAPSODICS *(Bartok)*---solo.
*BACCANALE *(Riegger)*---group.
DOLOROSA *(Villa-Lobos)*---solo.

14th New York Concert---April 19, 1931. Guild Theatre.

120

15th New York Concert---December 6, 1931.
Martin Beck Theatre.

*DITHYRAMBIC *(Copland)*---solo.
*SERENADE *(Schoenberg)*---solo.
*INCANTATION *(Villa-Lobos)*---solo.

16th New York Concert---Jan. 31, 1932. Guild Theatre.

17th New York Concert---Feb. 28, 1932. Guild Theatre.

*CEREMONIALS *(Engel)*---group.

18th New York Concert---April 3, 1932. Guild Theatre.

19th New York Concert---Nov. 20, 1932. Guild Theatre.

*SATYRIC FESTIVAL SONG *(Weisshaus)*---solo.
*PRELUDE *(Chavez)*---solo.

20th New York Concert---November 29, 1932.
New School for Social Research.

21st New York Concert---March 18, 1933.
McMillin Theatre.

22nd New York Concert---May 4, 1933. Guild Theatre.
*EKSTASIS *(Engel)*---solo.

23rd New York Concert---Feb. 18, 1934. Guild Theatre.

*FRENETIC RHYTHMS (Three dances of possession)
(Riegger)---solo.

121

*Transitions---*a.* Prologue; *b.* Sarabande; *c.* Panto-
mime; *d.* Epilogue *(Engel)*---solo.

24th New York Concert---Feb. 25, 1934. Guild Theatre.
*Celebration *(Horst)*---group.
*Four Casual Developments *(Cowell)*---group.

25th New York Concert---April 22, 1934. Alvin Theatre.
*Integrales *(Varese)*---group.

**26th and 27th New York Concerts---Nov. 11-18, 1934.
Guild Theatre.**
*Dance in Four Parts *(Antheil)*---solo.
*American Provincials---*a.* Act of Piety (solo); *b.* Act
of Judgment (group)---*(Horst)*.

28th New York Concert---Feb. 10, 1935. Guild Theatre.
*Praeludium *(Nordoff)*---solo.
*Course *(Antheil)*---group.

29th New York Concert---Mar. 2, 1935. McMillin Theatre.

30th New York Concert---April 28, 1935. Guild Theatre.
*Frontier *(Horst)*---solo.

**31st and 32nd New York Concerts---November 10-17,
1935. Guild Theatre.**
*Imperial Gesture *(Engel)*---solo.

122

**33rd and 34th New York Concerts---Feb. 23, Mar. 1, 1936.
Guild Theatre.**

*HORIZONS *(Horst)*---group.

**35th and 36th New York Concerts---Dec. 20 and 27, 1936.
Guild Theatre.**

*CHRONICLE *(Riegger)*---group.

**37th and 38th New York Concerts---March 2 and 4, 1937.
Guild Theatre.**

39th New York Concert---May 2, 1937. Guild Theatre.

*Indicates a first Performance of Dance

OTHER COMPLETE NEW YORK CONCERTS

40: March 21, 1930. Washington Irving High School.
41: March 20, 1931. Washington Irving High School.
42: March 26, 1932. Washington Irving High School.
43: Feb. 5, 1933. Guild Theatre.
44: Feb. 12, 1933. Guild Theatre.
45: Feb. 24, 1933. Brooklyn Academy of Music.
46: March 25, 1933. Washington Irving High School.
47: March 31, 1934. Washington Irving High School.
48: March 23, 1935. Washington Irving High School.
49: Dec. 11, 1935. Brooklyn Academy of Music.
50: Jan. 5, 1936. Y. M. H. A.
51: Feb. 15, 1936. Washington Irving High School.
52: Jan. 10, 1937. Y. M. H. A.
53: Feb. 6, 1937. Washington Irving High School.

CONCERT TOURS

1. May 27, 1926   Kilbourn Hall, Rochester, N. Y.
2. 3. 4.   Peterborough, N. H., Mariarden
     Aug. 20-21, 1926   Theatre (3)
5. Feb. 4, 1928   Danbury, Conn., H. S. Auditorium
6. Jan. 24, 1929   Bennett School, Millbrook, N. Y.
7. Feb. 18, 1929   Sage Hall, Northampton, Mass.
8. Jan. 16, 1930   Springer Opera House, Columbus, Ga.
9. Jan. 18, 1930   Institute Chapel, Tuskegee, Ala.
10. Jan. 20, 1930   Gulf Park College, Gulfport, Miss.
11. Feb. 10, 1930   South Side Jr. H. S., Watertown, N. Y.
12. Feb. 11, 1930   Jr. H. S. Auditorium,
     Amsterdam, N. Y.
13. Feb. 28, 1930   Arts Club, Chicago, Ill.
14. Mar. 29, 1930   Bennett School, Millbrook, N. Y.
15. June 2, 1930   Met. Theatre, Seattle, Wash.
16. June 16, 1930   Cornish School, Seattle, Wash.
17. Dec. 1, 1930   Jewish Com. Center, Jersey City, N. J.
18. Mar. 18, 1931   Century Club, Scranton, Pa.
19. May 28, 1931   Lydia Mendelssohn Theatre,
     Ann Arbor, Mich.
20. Jan. 22, 1932   National Theatre, Washington, D. C.
21. Feb. 4, 1932   F. S. C. W., Tallahassee, Fla.
22. Feb. 5, 1932   Town Theatre, Columbia, S. C.

23.	Feb. 6, 1932	Winthrop College, Rock Hill, S. C.
24.	Apr. 8, 1932	Jordan Hall, Boston, Mass.
25.	Apr. 9, 1932	Ethel Walker School, Simsbury, Conn.
26.	Apr. 11, 1932	The Womans Club, Richmond, Va.
27.	Apr. 12, 1932	The Manor Club, Pelham Manor, N.Y.
28. 29.		Lydia Mendelssohn Theatre,
	June 2-3, 1932	Ann Arbor, Mich. (2)
30.	Nov. 1, 1932	Clark University, Worcester, Mass.
31.	Nov. 15, 1932	Broad St. Theatre, Philadelphia, Pa.
32.	Nov. 21, 1932	Woman's College, Greensboro, N. C.
33.	Nov. 23, 1932	Randolph-Macon College,
		Lynchburg, Va.
34.	Nov. 24, 1932	The Chapel, Sweet Briar, Va.
35.	Feb. 20, 1933	Y. M. H. A., Newark, N. J.
36.	Feb. 26, 1933	Bonstelle Theatre, Detroit, Mich.
37.	Mar. 13, 1933	Bennington College, Bennington, Vt.
38.	Apr. 24, 1933	Jewish Com. Center, Jersey City, N. J.
39.	Oct. 17, 1933	Colgate University, Hamilton, N. Y.
40.	Nov. 22, 1933	Greene Hall, Northampton, Mass.
41.	Mar. 13, 1934	Massey Hall, Toronto, Canada
42.	July 20, 1934	Bennington College, Bennington, Vt.
43.	Jan. 14, 1935	Bellevue-Stratford, Philadelphia, Pa.
44.	Mar. 7, 1935	Conn. College, New London, Conn.
45.	Mar. 13, 1935	Rockford Theatre, Rockford, Ill.
46.	Mar. 15, 1935	Principia, St. Louis, Mo.
47.	Mar. 18, 1935	Ohio Wesleyan University,

48. Mar. 21, 1935   Delaware, O.
49. Mar. 27, 1935   Joslyn Memorial, Omaha, Neb.
50. 51.   Theatre, Springfield, Mass.
    Aug. 14-15, 1935   Vermont State Armory,
                       Bennington, Vt. (2)
52. Aug. 18, 1935   Town Hall, Peterboro, N. H.
53. Dec. 6, 1935   State T. C. Auditorium, Buffalo, N. Y.
54. Jan. 17, 1936   Rollins College, Winter Park, Fla.
55. Feb. 3, 1936   Plantations Club, Providence, R. I.
56. Feb. 5, 1936   Repertory Theatre, Boston, Mass.
57. Mar. 15, 1936   Bloomfield Hills, Mich.,
                       Kingswood School
58. Mar. 16, 1936   Detroit, Mich., Orchestra Hall
59. Mar. 20, 1936   Seattle, Wash., Moore Theatre
60. Mar. 23, 1936   Portland, Ore., Auditorium
61. Mar. 24, 1936   Tacoma, Wash., Jason Lee Auditorium
62. Mar. 27, 1936   Oakland, Cal., Auditorium
63. Mar. 28, 1936   Carmel, Cal., Sunset H. S.
64. Mar. 30, 1936   San Francisco, Calif., Opera House
65. Apr. 1, 1936   San Jose, Calif., State College
66. Apr. 2, 1936.   Palo Alto, Calif., Stanford University
67. Apr. 4, 1936   Santa Barbara, Calif., Lobero Theatre
68. Apr. 7, 1936   Los Angeles, Calif., Philharmonic
                       Auditorium
69. Apr. 10, 1936   Los Angeles, Calif., Philharmonic
                       Auditorium

70.	Apr. 21, 1936	Colorado Springs, Colo., Fine Arts Center
71.	Apr. 22, 1936	Colorado Springs, Colo., Fine Arts Center
72.	Apr. 26, 1936	Chicago, Ill., Studebaker Theatre
73.	Apr. 28, 1936	Oxford, O., Western College
74. 75.	July 31-Aug. 1, 1936	Bennington College, Bennington, Vt. (2)
76.	Nov. 19, 1936	Bennington College, Bennington, Vt.
77.	Mar. 12, 1937	Madison, Wis., Parkway Theatre
78.	Mar. 14, 1937	Chicago, Ill., Auditorium
79.	Mar. 19, 1937	Billings, Mont., State Normal School
80.	Mar. 31, 1937	Vancouver, B. C., Empress Theatre
81.	April 1, 1937	Tacoma, Wash., Jason Lee Auditorium
82.	April 3, 1937	Seattle, Wash., Moore Theatre
83.	April 8, 1937	San Francisco, Calif., Opera House
84.	April 11, 1937	San Francisco, Calif., Opera House
85.	April 10, 1937	Carmel, Calif., Sunset H. S.
86.	April 13, 1937	Santa Barbara, Calif., Lobero Theatre
87.	April 16, 1937	Los Angeles, Calif., Auditorium
88.	April 20, 1937	Denton, Texas, T. S. C. W. Auditorium
89.	April 23, 1937	Tallahassee, Fla., College Auditorium
90.	April 26, 1937	Lynchburg, Va., Randolph-Macon College
91.	April 30, 1937	Pittsburgh, Pa., Carnegie Music Hall

127

SPECIAL EVENTS

April 26, 27, 28, 1929. Manhattan Opera House, New York.

Danced principle role (with Charles Weidman) in Richard Strauss' "Ein Heldenleben", presented by the Neighborhood Playhouse under the direction of Irene Lewisohn with the Cleveland Symphony Orchestra, Nikolai Sokoloff conducting.

Feb. 20, 21, 22, 1930. Mecca Auditorium, New York.

Danced principal role (with Charles Weidman) in Charles Martin Loeffler's "Pagan Poem", presented by the Neighborhood Playhouse under the direction of Irene Lewisohn with the Cleveland Symphony Orchestra, Nikolai Sokoloff conducting.

April 11, 12 and 14, 1930. Metropolitan Opera House, Philadelphia, Pa.

April 22 and 23, 1930. Metropolitan Opera House, New York.

Danced principal role (The Chosen One) in Igor Stravinsky's "Le Sacre du Printemps", with the Philadelphia Symphony Orchestra, Leopold Stokowski conducting.

Apeared with Blanche Yurka in Sophocles' "Electra" at Ann Arbor Dramatic Festival. Week of May 25, 1931, and on tour.

Was granted the first Fellowship to a dancer by the John Simon Guggenheim Memorial Foundation. March, 1932.

Appeared on Inaugural Program of Radio City Music Hall (Rockefeller Center, New York City). Dec. 27, 1932.

First performance of Tragic Pattern --- (Chorus of Furies) --- (Horst) --- group.

Assisted Katharine Cornell and Guthrie McClintic in the production of Andre Obey's "Lucrece" Belasco Theatre. Jan. 1933.

Produced Six Miracle Plays for Stage Alliance at Guild Theatre. Feb. 5 and 12, 1933.

Directed dances for Katharine Cornell's production of "Romeo and Juliet". Nov., 1934.

Appointed by Mayor La Guardia to Municipal Art Committee. Jan., 1935.

Directed the Movement for Archibald Macleish's play "Panic", Imperial Theatre. March 14-15, 1935.

Produced first Workshop Production of the Bennington School of the Dance, Bennington, Vt. Aug. 14-15, 1935.

First performance of Panorama --- (Lloyd) group.

Danced for President and Mrs. Roosevelt at The White House. Feb. 26, 1937.

March and April, 1936. First trans-continental tour in solo recitals.

March, April, May, 1937. Second trans-continental tour with group of 12.

ACKNOWLEDGMENTS

Acknowledgment is made to the following individuals and publications for the material listed below:

John Martin - - - Dance Critic of the New York Times. New York Times, March, 1929; Feb., 1931; May, 1933; Nov., 1933; Nov., 1934; March, 1934; April, 1934; Nov., 1935; March, 1936; Aug., 1936; Aug., 1937.

AFFIRMATIONS

Lydia Barton, Stage and Screen, Feb., 1926; New York Telegram, April 19, 1926; Francis McClarnan Kemp, Dance Magazine, March, 1927; W. Adolphe Roberts, Dance Magazine, Aug., 1928; Beth Buchanan, New York Evening World, Feb. 2, 1930; Michigan Daily, Ann Arbor, May 20, 1931; Trend--- Vol. 1, 1932; Elizabeth McClausland, Springfield, Mass., Repulican, April 30, 1933; Jewish Daily Bulletin, New York, Feb. 18, 1934; Dance Observer, April, 1934; New York Mirror, Feb. 8, 1935; American Dancer, April, 1935; The News, Santa Barbara, Calif., Sept. 18, 1935, April 13, 1937; Santa Barbara Press, Santa Barbara, Calif., Sept. 22, 1935; Christian Science Monitor, Nov. 26, 1935, March 17, 1936; Boston Transcript, Feb. 1, 1936; Boston Herald, Feb. 5, 1936; Boot and Shoe Recorder, Feb. 29, 1936; San Francisco News, March 27, 1936; Herald Express, Los Angeles, March 28, 1936; Stanford Daily, April 1, 1936; The Post, Washington, D.C., Oct.

16, 1936; Washington News, Washington, D.C., Dec. 26, 1936; World-Telegram, New York, Dec. 26, 1936; American Arts Monthly, Sept., 1936.

Biography of Martha Graham   -   -   -   Winthrop Sargeant
The Dance Observer, May 1934-1937

Relation of Music to Movement   -   -   -   -   Margaret Lloyd
Christian Science Monitor, March 3, 1932

Martha Graham   -   -   -   -   -   -   -   -   -   -   Stark Young
The New Republic, December 14, 1932

The Foreword by Merle Armitage, and the articles by Lincoln Kerstein, Evangeline Stowkowski, Wallingford Reigger, Edith J. R. Isaacs, Roy Hargrave, James Johnson Sweeney, George Anthiel, Martha Graham, and Louis Danz were written especially for this book.

The thirteen ink drawings for chapter headings by Carlos Dyer were made for this Volume.

Photographs by Pinchot, Morgan, Sunami.

End paper photographs by: Front, Sunami; Back, Tucker.

Action photographs by Hansen, Tucker, Bouchard.

Oil painting of Martha Graham by Edward Biberman.

Water color tempera painting of "Lamentation" by Carlos Dyer.

Caricature by Fruhauf.

Musical score of "Pioneer" by Louis Horst.

Space diagrams by Arch Lauterer.

Research, Louis Horst and Ramiel McGehee.

The special contributions of Ramiel McGehee for his insight into sources and his suggestions in shaping materials is gratefully acknowledged.

What is Form?
Form is the
Memory of Spiritual
Content. When
do Form and
Content Meet?
Form and Content
meet in Action